THE NEW
FEMINIZED MAJORITY

HOW DEMOCRATS CAN CHANGE AMERICA
WITH WOMEN'S VALUES

KATHERINE ADAM AND CHARLES DERBER

Paradigm Publishers
Boulder • London

Paradigm Publishers is committed to preserving ancient forests and natural resources. We elected to print *The New Feminized Majority* on 50% post consumer recycled paper, processed chlorine free. As a result, for this printing, we have saved:

8 Trees (40' tall and 6-8" diameter)
3,436 Gallons of Wastewater
1,382 Kilowatt Hours of Electricity
378 Pounds of Solid Waste
744 Pounds of Greenhouse Gases

Paradigm Publishers made this paper choice because our printer, Thomson-Shore, Inc., is a member of Green Press Initiative, a nonprofit program dedicated to supporting authors, publishers, and suppliers in their efforts to reduce their use of fiber obtained from endangered forests.

For more information, visit www.greenpressinitiative.org

Copyright © 2008 Paradigm Publishers

Published in the United States by Paradigm Publishers, 3360 Mitchell Lane Suite E, Boulder, CO 80301 USA.

Paradigm Publishers is the trade name of Birkenkamp & Company, LLC, Dean Birkenkamp, President and Publisher.

Library of Congress Cataloging-in-Publication Data is available.

ISBN 978-1-59451-567-5 (hc)
ISBN 978-1-59451-568-2 (pbk)

Printed and bound in the United States of America on acid-free paper that meets the standards of the American National Standard for Permanence of Paper for Printed Library Materials.

Designed and typeset by Straight Creek Bookmakers.

12 11 10 09 08   1 2 3 4 5

*To my mother, who taught me
the importance of values
—Katherine Adam*

*To Katherine's generation,
which gives me hope for a better world
—Charles Derber*

Contents

Democrats Have Values, Too

On a rainy night in early November 2004, thousands of Democrats stood shivering in a downtown Boston square, waiting for a victory speech that never came. Meanwhile, hundreds of befuddled journalists huddled in tents in the area's periphery, contemplating how their networks' exit polls proved to be so wrong. And in a hotel room overlooking the whole scene, a presidential campaign staff wondered when they should accept defeat.

Finally, the bad news came. The major news networks began to project that Ohio would go red, and that George W. Bush had won a second term as president. Democratic hearts collectively sank. Kerry supporters slowly filed out of the packed outdoor "victory party" to catch cabs home, their clothes soaked by rain and their cheeks wet with tears.

The look on many of these Bostonians' faces could only be described as "dazed." For them—and for progressive thinkers around the country—feelings of disappointment and dread mixed with a deep sense of confusion. After four years of divisive "Leave No Millionaire Behind" domestic policies and a quagmire in Iraq, the Bush administration still managed to convince a majority of American voters that the Republican Party best represented their interests.

In Fort Lauderdale, Florida, the Reverend D. James Kennedy was celebrating. As the founder of Coral Ridge

1

Ministries and a vocal member of the political Christian Right, he certainly supported George W. Bush's reelection bid. Bush's first term led to major gains for Christian conservatives, and his second term seemed even more promising. In this election, voters had given Bush a "moral mandate," Kennedy told the Associated Press. "Now that values voters have delivered for George Bush, he must deliver for their values."[1] Indeed, the self-proclaimed values voters turned out for Bush in a big way: the president received the support of 78 percent of evangelicals, which represented 23 percent of total voters.[2]

While Democrats fiercely and loudly courted new voters through organizations like MoveOn.org and America Coming Together, the Bush campaign quietly worked with religious groups around the country to register new evangelical voters and ensure they came to the polls. On Bush's last day of campaigning in November 2004, he held a rally in Ohio—a state the campaign hoped would bring big evangelical numbers for Bush. Ohio ended up securing the Republican victory. That same evening, it was also one of eleven states to pass a bill banning same-sex marriage.[3] Republicans had successfully motivated the social conservatives, a strategy that produced palpable results. Whereas Christian beliefs historically had little bearing on partisan identity, more than 75 percent of evangelical Christians now consider themselves Republicans.[4]

The impact of Bush's strategy goes far beyond the 2004 presidential election. Republicans created a much larger movement of values-based voting. The millions of evangelicals who turned out for George W. Bush voted for him not because they thought his policies would significantly improve their lives; they cast their votes based on their religious identity, even when Bush's policies would hit them in their own pocketbooks. Evangelicals have a certain view of how the world *should* be, based on their Christian values. They vote for the candidates who they feel will bring the country more in line with this general worldview. In the aftermath of the election, America witnessed the passion of evangelical activists who felt the Bush win as a crucial step in creating a more virtuous world. Dennis Prager, a Christian radio commentator, described how "civilization as we understand it was in the balance" in the election, and proclaimed that "a beautiful man has been vindicated."[5] The Bush campaign had succeeded in casting Bush as a redeemer of traditional morality who would use his steadfast values to save America from itself.

The Kerry campaign had a different strategy to win. Following the lead of Bill Clinton in the 1996 election, the Kerry campaign employed a "triangulation" strategy, meant to give the candidate broad-based appeal. The strategy included moving to the right on a number of issues in an effort to pick up Independents and undecided voters. Yet, because Kerry lacked the dynamism and political acumen of Clinton, his attempt at this strategy seemed insincere and strangely comical. Pundits skewered Kerry when he claimed he actually voted for the $87 billion appropriation bill for Iraq and Afghanistan *before* he voted against it. Even Independents, the 26 percent of voters who were supposed to respond most strongly to the triangulation strategy, ended up splitting their votes between the two candidates.[6]

As much as political pundits have berated Kerry for his personal mistakes, the Bush/Cheney win was actually the result of years of poor strategy by the Democrats. To fulfill its goals of triangulation, the Democratic Party had spent the Clinton years confusing voters about its ideals. Clinton masterfully moved around the ideological spectrum, tightening gun control to please liberals, and changing welfare to appease conservatives. It worked well for Clinton, who was reelected and had high approval ratings. In the long run, however, Democrats were faced with a problem: Voters had no idea what the Democratic Party was about. Republicans, meanwhile, created a larger and more forward-thinking strategy based on identity and values. And, while the Democrats triangulated to the right, the Republican strategy did not rely on moving left.

Triangulation led Democrats to abandon their populist agenda. They pursued policies of fiscal conservatism so as not to be seen as supporting "big government." The party embraced a new paradigm of economic elitism and faced a credibility gap when it fought the Bush administration's tax cuts for the rich and provoucher education program. In the end, the Republican Party deflected any criticism for its divisive antipopulist economic policies and ensured that the political conversation focused on cultural issues in a values framework.

Although some strategists have encouraged the Democratic Party to adopt a progressive values platform, most of the party seems unconvinced that running campaigns based on generalized values is the key to success. Many leading Democrats even feel that Democratic losses are the result of not triangulating *enough*, and they urge candidates to push even more conservative positions on social and military issues. The most misinformed Democrats, however, believe that a moral values approach to politics in America can never exist outside of a Christian or religious framework. These Democrats are not only wrong but also a dangerous influence on the rest of the party. If Democrats refuse to start looking at issues in a values framework they will squander an opportunity to lead America into a new era of progressivism.

Gender, Values, and the Democrats

As the only group targeted by a political party using a value-based strategy, evangelicals are seen as the only people who match their actions and politics to their values. Values, however, are a universal human phenomenon. In their simplest form, values are socially constructed views about how the world should be. In 1651, Thomas Hobbes wrote about the subjectivity of values and how we shape our values to fit our ideas of what makes a perfect society.

> But whatsoever is the object of any man's appetite or desire, that it is which he for his part calleth "good"; and the object of his contempt "vile" and "inconsiderable." For these words of good, evil, and contemptible, are ever used with relation to the person that useth them. There being nothing simply and absolutely so; nor any common rule of Good or Evil, to be taken from the nature of the objects themselves.[7]

Looking past Hobbes's notorious pessimism about the human condition, this idea highlights that everyone acts on values and that values are socially constructed. Therefore, values vary from person to person, and a person has the ability to change his or her values.

Although Hobbes refers to an individual's values, his message translates to larger community values. Americans, for example, hold American values. Every political candidate, on the right or the left, knows that most Americans respond favorably to the idea that a person should be rewarded for hard work. This is a capitalist, American value. Members of other societies might feel that a person should be rewarded for his or her skin color or family bloodline. Every person is socialized into the values of his or her community or nation, and these values then intersect with other values the person has, such as those based his or her religion, race, and socioeconomic class.

Perhaps the most important set of socialized values, however, is based on a person's gender. We term these values *feminized values* and *masculinized values*. In this book, we will outline how men's and women's different value systems create divergent views about what America should be. We argue that Americans carry gendered attitudes into the voting booth and, like the evangelicals, vote based on how these values translate to specific political issues.

Just as some groups' values fall to the more conservative end of the political spectrum, other groups' values fall to the left. Evangelicals usually support right-wing candidates, because their moral values are highly conservative. We will introduce a group of voters whose values reflect progressive ideals: feminized values voters. If evangelicals represent the key to Republican electoral victory, then feminized values voters represent the chance for Democrats to usher in a new progressive era.

Feminized values are the values into which women are socialized; a majority of women hold these values, as do a smaller percentage of men, for reasons we will describe shortly. The potential for a more progressive era arises because the women and men who hold feminized values make up today a majority of the country and of voters.

We term feminized values voters the *feminized majority*. These women and men will not only change election outcomes, but also will transform American values and the American Dream. The feminized majority supports a strong welfare state, views social issues through a lens of egalitarianism, and feels that government should do more in general to help its most vulnerable citizens. Feminized majority voters support stem-cell research, comprehensive sex education, and environmental protection. They reject violent imperialism. They worry about their long-term economic security and fear that neither party will provide them with adequate health care. In a much deeper and richer way than American masculinized voters, the feminized majority yearns for a progressive, populist America.

We call these voters the feminized majority because the values they carry truly are becoming majoritarian. We will describe the political and economic changes that have led to this point. It is important to remember that

President Bush changed the 2004 election by mobilizing evangelicals, who represent only 23 percent of voters. Now, Democrats have the opportunity to change America in dramatic ways with the support of a much larger part of the electorate. While the general perception is that the United States is a conservative country, we shall show that feminized values are held by an increasingly robust majority of voters in the country who are prepared to support a progressive politics of social justice.

The Democrats can lead the feminized majority if they are willing to abandon their triangulation strategy and create a values-based platform. This approach seems unorthodox, because we usually conflate values and morals with religion and conservatism. However, values are nothing more than socially constructed ideals that provide a moral compass for each person, regardless of where he or she falls on the political spectrum. Once Democrats recognize the power of values in elections, they can begin appealing to values voters.

The 2008 presidential election cycle is the perfect time for Democrats to form a relationship with the feminized majority. Hillary Clinton, the likely Democratic nominee at this writing, has a long history as an advocate for feminized issues. Being a woman, she symbolizes the gendered nature of the rising feminized majority. Hillary is a contradictory candidate, with masculinized as well as feminized profiles, and far from the most feminized of the candidates in 2008. But the Clinton campaign could become a turning point in American history, and Democrats should use this opportunity to develop a feminized values vision and platform.

Contradictions and Caveats

The argument in this book may seem counterintuitive to many readers. We live in dangerous times. Since 9/11, a defining event of the new twenty-first century, the majority of Americans are newly concerned with national security and their own safety. The attacks on New York and Washington, the first foreign attacks on the American mainland for almost 200 years, killed nearly 3,000 innocent civilians and made it clear that every American is now a potential target.

To some, this does not seem an opportune moment for feminized politics. Global turbulence and threats of attacks create fear, stoked sometimes into mass hysteria by political parties that see partisan advantage in exploiting it. As fear ratchets up with color-coded alarms and newspaper images of subway bombs killing commuters in Madrid and London, so too does the desire for protection. Traditionally, it is strong men—soldiers, generals, and political leaders—who protect the country, in the name of masculine honor, responsibility, and patriotism.

Since 9/11, George W. Bush made the war on terrorism his main issue. Most analysts believe that Bush won reelection in 2004 on the claim that only Republicans will build the overwhelming military strength and power necessary to keep Americans safe. Republicans present this as the ultimate moral issue in their masculinized politics. National security requires men willing to fight and sacrifice for the country. Without saying so explicitly, they suggest that Democrats—dovish, intellectual, and lacking in traditional masculine values—are too feminized to lead the country in an age of terrorism.

Military strength has always been a pillar of masculinized politics. In America, the world's only superpower, it can make feminized politics appear almost comic. The 1988 campaign image of Democratic nominee Michael Dukakis—short, cerebral, and looking almost ridiculous sitting in a tank—captured precisely what the Republicans saw as their ticket to victory. Democrats were too weak, essentially too womanly, to lead the country in the cold war—and Bush won a landslide victory over Dukakis.

It is easy to conclude that feminized politics cannot gain traction in America. It is a serious issue, and we take it seriously in this book. Feminized politics is not a politics of weakness, but it offers a different model of strength and security. Throughout the book, we return to this question, exploring how feminized Democratic politicians approach issues of national security and offer strategic examples of success for new, less-militarized visions and strategies.

This is part of a larger historical riddle about the viability of feminized politics in one of the world's most masculinized countries. In Chapter 2, we show that America developed historically in a masculinized model, with masculine values shaping most of our institutions and ideology throughout the nineteenth and twentieth centuries. A shift to feminized values and politics is thus a sea change, not only in foreign policy but also in domestic affairs and in the American Dream itself. In Chapter 3 and subsequent chapters, we show the fitful rise and spread of feminized values in this deeply masculinized nation, and the many challenges the rising feminized majority faces as it contends with deeply entrenched masculinized power and morality.

Three other important caveats should be mentioned. While this book focuses on values, we recognize that voters vote their interests as well as their moral concerns. A key goal of feminized politics today is achieving universal health care, which feminized voters support because it expresses their moral focus on equality, inclusiveness, and community. But many also support it because they can't pay for their own health care and are acting out of self-interest.

Our focus on values does not reduce interests to a secondary force in politics. Instead, most voters see their interests as part of a broader vision of how to organize a good society. We view values not as a "higher" or more idealistic politics, but one that always serves to help focus and crystallize interests, either of particular groups or of the whole society. Some voters may only vote narrow self-interest without reference to any moral compass, and many others may vote for their own interests in contradiction to their own values. We pay close attention to the relation between values and interests, showing that feminized values are a way to organize large sectors of the population to achieve both their moral concerns and their own economic and social interests.

This leads to a second point about why we call the politics we advocate "feminized." Some might say we are simply discussing what should be called progressive politics. Universal heath care, for example, is typically described as a progressive goal. To describe it as a feminized goal may seem to imply that it serves only women or is supported only by them. Moreover, it appears to privilege women's concerns over those of racial minorities or the poor or the working class.

We address these legitimate concerns throughout the book. We do not believe that women's needs trump those of the working class or racial minorities, and we do not see feminized politics as addressing only the concerns of women. A distinctive characteristic of feminized values, which are held mainly by women but also by millions of men, is that they aim to help the entire community. Universal health care serves everyone's interests but it is a political goal reflecting feminized values and is supported more by women than men. To call it feminized affirms the political clout of the new feminized majority and shows that feminized voters will be the majority bloc supporting progressive political change. Feminized politics is an American approach to creating a democratic agenda, and the complexities of the relation between gender and class politics are one of our most important themes.

The feminized majority differs from the group that progressive thinkers have historically envisioned as the agent of change. Progressives have often viewed the constituency for progressive social change as the lower and working classes represented by unions and labor parties as in Europe. But while class divisions and economic inequalities are increasingly acute in the United States and urgently need remedy, the base for class change in the country lies, paradoxically, in a group bridging different classes and united by values rooted in gender. This reflects not only the universal importance of gendered values but also the weakness and fragmentation of working-class culture in America.

Americans have learned to see *feminist* politics as a form of identity politics to advance women's interests. But while some feminists and feminist organizations fit that bill, our analysis suggests a different understanding of *feminized* values and voters. The political attitudes and behavior of the feminized majority show that the base for progressive change in America crosses class lines. Its largest constituency is working-class and poor women. But it includes many middle- and upper-middle-class values voters, including millions of females and many males who vote against their own class interests to support their feminized values. Our analysis points to a new political view of the relation between gender and class, and a new strategy to achieve progressive change in America.

This leads to our final and critically important caveat. We offer, here, a new "feminized frame" for analyzing politics in America. Our frame is a new moral lens, distinguishing between feminized and masculinized political values and visions. Our "feminized" framing is very closely related to certain forms of feminism, as we discuss in Chapter 5, but is not identical to a "feminist" frame as usually conceived, although both are rooted in gender and both are concerned with rights of women. A "feminized" political vision is rooted in values held more often by women and integral to the culture in which women are socialized in a given historical era. But the overlap between feminized values, as we use the term, and various feminist movements is an empirical question. Feminist movements that focus only on women's rights—or on white or middle-class women's concerns—are not necessarily advancing what we call here a feminized politics. Nonetheless, many core feminized values, such as equality, have grown out of the role of feminist movements in championing equality for women and other groups.

A feminized politics promotes a specific set of values linked to women's heritage and contemporary position in a particular society. In the United States today, it is a politics of equality and peace, empathy, and community. It is a universalistic politics, advancing the rights of women, minorities, the environment and, most important, the interests of society as a whole. In Chapter 1, we introduce the distinction in America today between feminized and masculinized values. In the chapters that follow, we elaborate on this distinction, and in Chapter 5, we explicitly spell out the overlap and differences between "feminized" and various "feminist" frames.

A Road Map

This book provides the first portrait of the new feminized majority and demonstrates how it can become the foundation of an enduring Democratic Party majority that can change the nation. We offer a two part argument: (1) voters with feminized values have become a majority in the country, and (2) the Democratic Party can become a lasting governing party and achieve major progressive change if it mobilizes the new feminized majority as its own base.

The arguments and data we report show that, contrary to common wisdom, the majority of Americans are progressive on both domestic and foreign policy issues. Elites in both political parties are far more conservative than the feminized majority. Our key argument is that the Democrats can become a governing party only by becoming a voice of this new majoritarian feminized constituency. But this requires understanding the values and mind-set of the feminized majority and then catalyzing the Democratic Party to enact the changes wanted by the feminized majority.

In Chapters 1–5, we look at the rise and spread of feminized values. We describe America's development as a masculinized country and the historical conditions giving rise in recent decades to the new feminized majority. We also draw a detailed picture of the feminized majority itself: who make it up, what are its values, and what is its vision of the country. We look closely at the relation between gender and class, exploring how the feminized majority can be a "carrier" of class politics.

In Chapters 6–10, we identify a Democratic Party strategy for victory based on feminized politics and grassroots movements rooted in the feminized majority. We argue that Democrats need to develop a moral vision addressed to the feminized majority, one that can make the feminized majority a loyal base of the party. We show that the feminized majority is much larger than the Christian conservative base of the Republican Party and includes many Independents as well as registered Democrats. We identify the specific steps Democrats must take—in 2008 and beyond—to develop a successful relationship with this vast new majority.

We also discuss the hurdles and contradictions of this approach. The Democrats will have to transform their identity as a corporate party, as well as attract men to what, at first blush, may appear a violation of their own identity. It must also persuasively address the national security issues for both men and women. Finally, we will delve into the 2008 presidential election and beyond, paying special attention to Hillary Clinton's campaign and to key grassroots social movements that embrace feminized populist values.

The Democratic Party can become the governing party in the coming generation if it succeeds in aligning itself with and mobilizing the feminized majority. And the future of America will be bright if it embraces the feminized values of this new "moral majority."

Chapter One

Mars versus Venus

If the 2004 election proved anything, religion shapes values. Millions of evangelicals volunteered for the Bush campaign and voted for Bush in 2004 because they felt he truly understood their values and would support policy upholding these values. For evangelicals, the Bible provides an orienting influence, helping them to make decisions that they feel are in line with God. Even non-Christians often think of values and religion as synonymous. Americans, in particular, take this idea for granted. Many Americans would find it difficult to answer the question, "Do people hold values that are not related to religion?"

Though it may seem strange to remove values from the context of religion, values *do* emerge from secular sources and are created and re-created by cultures in different ways. Values differ based on a culture's political and economic systems, and its history. In every culture, however, people are socialized into a set of values based on their gender. Gender often determines a person's role in the culture and in the family. He or she then develops values that reflect this role. As cultures change and roles are reevaluated, the values associated with a person's gender also change. Nevertheless, gendered values are always an important influence on people's decisions, including their political opinions.

The idea that men and women carry different values is nothing new. In fact, men's and women's different values are the basis of the most popular relationship book ever published: *Men Are from Mars, Women Are from Venus.* With more than 14 million copies sold since its initial publication in 1992, the book's success shows that Americans feel the need for a better understanding of gendered values (and that they love self-help books).

Written by John Gray, a family therapist, the work asks readers to imagine that men and women originally inhabited two different planets, Mars and Venus. The Martians and Venusians eventually encountered each other and collectively fell in love. They decided to move to Earth—which was neutral territory—and live in harmony forever. As time went on, the Martians and Venusians developed a case of "selective amnesia" and "forgot they were from different planets and were supposed to be different."[1] Since this event, men and women have been in conflict. Women expect men to intuitively understand them and act like them, and vice versa. The key to saving relationships, therefore, is to examine the differences between men and women, and respect these differences.

Martians, for example, value "power, competency, efficiency, and achievement. They are always doing things to prove themselves and develop their power and skills. Their sense of self is defined through their ability to achieve results. They experience fulfillment primarily through success and accomplishment. Everything on Mars is a reflection of these values."[2]

Venusians, on the other hand, have different values. "They value love, communication, beauty, and relationships. They spend a lot of time supporting, helping, and nurturing one another. Their sense of self is defined through their feelings and the quality of their relationships. They experience fulfillment through sharing and relating."[3]

Men Are from Mars, Women Are from Venus validates something that seems intuitively true: A person's gender affects the way that he or she views the world. This simple fact is the first step toward understanding the feminized majority phenomenon. However, issues of gender are far more nuanced than the bipolar Martian and Venusian example. And as we will show, feminized and masculinized values certainly are not so simple.

There are two crucial differences between the Martian/Venusian assessment of gender and the feminized/masculinized approach we describe. First, the Mars and Venus metaphor implies that gendered values are in the DNA. After all, women are born Venusians, and men are born Martians. No Martian is capable of adopting the beliefs or qualities of a Venusian. There is no spectrum of Venusian and Martian values, and there is no way of reconciling a Martian identity with Venusian values. Because the purpose of *Men Are from Mars, Women Are from Venus* is to help readers in heterosexual relationships solve problems, the view that the difference of the sexes is part of nature rather than nurture is not important. However, as this book will show, the difference is critical in matters of politics. Feminized and masculinized values are created and re-created through socialization, not biology. A socialization approach to gendered values allows for variance and change.

The other difference between Martian and Venusian values and masculinized and feminized values is that Martians and Venusians were born into distinct value systems without the influence of the other gender. Martians and Venusians survived and thrived over time on different planets, never coming into contact with belief systems that were different from their own. When they fell in love with each other, their value systems were seen as equally important and given equal respect. As John Gray points out, relationship problems between the beings began only when they moved to Earth and forgot they were from different planets. Their underlying, poorly understood value differences causes them to butt heads. Each wants the other to adopt his or her values, but neither is very successful.

Feminized and masculinized values, however, were not created in isolation. Men and women have always been in contact with each other, and their value systems are created and re-created through their interactions. This is not to say that feminized and masculinized values are created in the same way. Men, who have traditionally held power in most societies, form value systems differently than women, who have traditionally been subjugated. Some writers even question whether women have any say in the values they carry. Existentialist philosopher and feminist Simone de Beauvoir writes, "In truth, women have never set up female values in opposition to male values; it is man who, desirous of maintaining masculine prerogatives, has invented that divergence."[4] To de Beauvoir, oppressed people do not create values—they are assigned them. We will explore how men's and women's different social roles in the United States have given them different value systems and led them to form different political opinions.

Naming Feminized and Masculinized Values

Feminized values are those in which women are socialized in a given time and place. In the United States, these contemporary values include *cooperation,* such as working together with others for a common good; *empathy,* or the ability to understand and be sensitive to what other people are feeling; *an appreciation for equality,* including the belief that everyone is entitled to certain rights; *a preference for nonviolent solutions to conflicts* and a belief that fighting only causes more problems; and *community,* or the feeling that everyone is a part of something bigger.

Men are socialized into what we call *masculinized val ues* that include *competitiveness,* or a desire to get ahead of others; *aggression,* or the need to maintain a tough demeanor; *individualism,* including the belief that everyone should make decisions based on what is best for him or her; and *a belief that violence is a necessary tool to solve problems,* or that fighting can be the best way to right a wrong. These values are expressed in everyday life—at work, with children, and in relationships. These values also relate to politics.

As the Mars and Venus metaphors suggest, women's values sharply contrast with the values held by a majority of men, reflecting the difference in the history and roles of the two sexes. Feminized values derive from the roles of caretaking and family nurturance that women were assigned historically, as well as the values of equality and community advanced by the modern feminist movement. All five feminized values reflect both traditional female subordination and the feminist struggle for equal rights. As we shall see, feminized values have become *universalistic values,* serving the well-being not just of women but society as a whole.

Until we become a culture with absolute gender equity, men and women will always be socialized into different kinds of values. However, the socialization process does not mean that all men or all women embrace the values of their gender. A person may adopt the values of the "opposite" gender. In fact, a polarized gender system is a distinctly heteronormative concept. Many communities around the world recognize multiple genders and view sexuality as a spectrum rather than a binary. America's views about gender are changing as well. Many progressive parents now seek to raise their children in a gender-neutral environment, viewing the gender binary as an outdated mechanism that stifles a child's self-actualization. When we examine gendered values, we must remember that men's and women's roles in society are shifting and not make the mistake of turning the two genders into exaggerated caricatures.

Furthermore, it is not necessary for a person to drastically reevaluate his or her gender identity to adopt values associated with the opposite gender. For example, men who tell their sons to "walk away" from people teasing them rather than swing a fist are not trying to make their sons "feminine" but are promoting their own individual values, which may be feminized because of their own biographies. A person's set of values is complex and nuanced and is created through his or her unique life experiences. Although a person is socialized into gendered values, a person's value system is shaped by many factors besides his or her gender, and a person's understanding of gender is shaped by factors other than his or her value system.

Some gender research reflects the nuances of gender identity, viewing masculinities and femininities as "projects to be accomplished in varying ways depending on the social context. Gender is produced differently among white blue-collar laborers, unemployed African Americans, white software developers, and black physicians."[5] A person's gendered values are constantly intersecting with the other values shaped by his or her background. This helps explain why 75 percent of women of color voted for John Kerry in 2004 compared to 44 percent of white women.[6] Women carry their gendered values into the voting booth, but only as a part of a larger identity.

Even with the variances created by race, socioeconomic class, region, religiosity, occupation, and age, gendered values still emerge as an important factor in the creation of a person's consciousness. In Chapter 4, we will show which values are associated with each gender, based on polling information. However, to help create a context for the poll data, let's first consider a master narrative: the cohesive, overarching principles that create the values of each gender. People with feminized values look at issues affecting their families and their communities with the goal of "together we can." These simple words sum up the importance of community, communication, cooperation, and collective aspirations. As Jean Baker Miller writes in her best-selling book, *Toward a New Psychology of Women* (1976), females are taught to value connections, nurturance, and interdependence. This reflects how women are assigned to be caretakers and to keep the family going and the community alive.

Those with masculinized values move through their lives with the feeling "alone I will." This shows their individualism and desire to be on top. Men learn to value the competition and dominance that will help them achieve success in business that capitalist society expects of them and that proves their masculinity.

Cognitive scientist and political analyst George Lakoff gives another version of a master narrative. In his book *Moral Politics* (1996), he argues that the reason liberals and conservatives have different worldviews is because they follow different models of morality. Conservatives carry a set of values stemming from a "strict father" model of morality. The underlying premise of this model is that people confront a dangerous world, one divided into good and evil. Survival in this dangerous world is a matter of moral will—those who are morally strong succeed. Moral strength comes through self-discipline. In this competitive system, those who do not succeed have only themselves to blame. Their failures, after all, indicate self-indulgence and a lack of self-discipline. Therefore, those who do not succeed in the system are morally weak.[7]

Liberals form opinions on issues in the framework of a "nurturant parent" model of morality. This model's foundation is that children learn to succeed through attachments to their parents. Ideally, children and their parents should have a loving and secure relationship. Children, out of love, will not want to disappoint their parents, and will work to live up to their parents' expectations. Happy children will be motivated to embody the traits of their parents, so parents must lead by example. Family dynamics should be based on mutual respect and empathy. Children will grow up to be self-conscious and caring adults. In order for this system to function, the world must be a nurturing place that encourages people to achieve their dreams. The system must help people along the way through interdependence and cooperation.[8]

A person's model of morality defines how he or she will perceive issues, and determines his or her reactions. Although Lakoff's morality models are not gendered, because he does not argue that the underlying American moral models arise from how men and women are socialized, his interpretation is still useful for understanding feminized and masculinized voters. Lakoff shows that people have master moral narratives and he helps explain how political differences reflect underlying value differences. He demonstrates the need for a values-driven politics. But he has not shown the historical and social roots of values, nor has he described how the larger power relations of society, including the class, race, or gender systems, are critical in creating each of our values. Most important, Lakoff ignores the fact that gender plays an increasingly important role in forming and changing American moral narratives. In short, he has not seen how the rise of feminized values and the feminized majority are transforming American values.

Understanding gendered values—and their relation to class struggles and an emancipatory human agenda—is the secret to a new American politics. It is also the key to a successful Democratic Party strategy. The Democratic Party has forgotten that Democrats have values too, and they have overlooked the rise of the feminized majority that is transforming American values right under their noses.

Together We Can and *Alone I Will* represent the underlying models that create feminized and masculinized values. The new feminized majority now creates the best opportunity for Democrats since the New Deal to set the agenda for the next generation. If Democrats can embrace this rising majority and champion the moral and policy agenda it seeks, the Democratic Party can lead America for decades in a new Democratic era. And, in conjunction with more visionary social movements awakened anew by Democratic victories, this new dynamic can help transform the country and the world, making a more peaceful, equitable, and sustainable planet.

CHAPTER TWO

America's Masculinized History

Masculinized values have ruled America since its founding. These values—which emphasize self-interest, competition, aggression, conquest, and winning—lie at the heart of the American Dream. They shaped the American sink-or-swim economy and helped fuel the constant, often violent, expansion that has created the American Empire. America's global military dominance, with more arms than all other countries put together, is the ultimate showcase of a historically masculinized America.

A brief sketch of American history shows that masculinized values and institutions have indelibly shaped our nation. These values appear in the rough, masculinized faces chiseled on Mount Rushmore; in the Robber Baron capitalists and imperial generals who have led corporations, the military, and both political parties; in the visions of Manifest Destiny that have moralized American empire building; in the Hollywood that lionized John Wayne and the cowboy-now-turned-action-hero; and in the social Darwinist ethos that has created the most masculinized capitalist system in the world.

To dislodge such deeply entrenched values and power is tantamount to a second American Revolution, and no revolution can succeed without understanding the history it is confronting. As we show in later chapters, subcurrents of feminized values and dreams—carried by social movements and sometimes the Democratic Party, as in the New Deal and the Great Society—have softened American history and seeded alternative American ideals, offering the rising feminized majority a historical footing to stand on. But in this chapter we show the hard truth that feminized politics faces in America: We live in a nation born and bred on masculinized values.

The nation's ruling classes and institutions—including most mainstream leaders of both the Republican and Democratic parties—have been at the forefront of this masculinized history. In the rest of this book, we show how a new breed of Democrats can change America by championing feminized values, and we look much more closely at the masculinized history of the party as well as its future. We predict that many leading mainstream Democrats as well as Republicans—both male and female—will resist and seek to repress the unexpected moral revolution carried by the rising feminized majority. And they will do so in the name of preserving America's most sacred values.

Their masculinized claim to America's moral legacy is not entirely spurious. The earliest settlers at Plymouth Rock brought over masculinized values. By the end of the nineteenth century, these values congealed in the reigning American myths and dreams that defined America itself.

Puritans, Founding Fathers, Frontiersmen, and Robber Barons

Protestant zealots settled America and brought a masculinized religious and economic dream. The Puritans who came over on the *Mayflower* were unabashed masculinized theocrats. Their religious doctrine was absolutist—based on a literal reading of the Bible as the word of God—and tolerated no dissent, leading more feminized settlers, such as Roger Williams and Anne Hutchison, to leave a theocratic Massachusetts to create a less authoritarian and more democratic Rhode Island.[1]

Puritan theocracy was harsh and hierarchical, requiring unquestioned submission to male religious leaders and a rigid concept of moral purity that condemned, among other things, dancing, music, and the maypole. The Puritans treated feminized sexuality, artistic expression, religious dissent, and critical thinking as satanic. The punishment, as the Salem witch trials suggested, could be threats of death or burning at the stake, a symbol of the masculinized aggression and violence at the heart of the Puritan moral code.[2]

Puritans moralized masculinized dominance as God's will. A 1636 rule prevented women from speaking in church to preserve the moral order. The Puritans treated masculinized control in the church, family, and politics as essential to protecting women, spirituality, and society itself. Males exercised control moralized as masculinized protection and honor in the service of God.[3]

The Puritans had an element of feminized morality in their idealization of Puritan community. Puritans were not the rugged individualists who later came to epitomize American masculinized values; the Puritans believed that moral perfection was embodied in communal life. But the male monopoly of power, ordained by God, enabled the Puritans to masculinize the feminized value of community. The Puritans treated their own community, in the famous words of John Winthrop, as a "shining city on the hill," giving themselves and America itself a moral basis for taking land, removing Indians, and beginning to build what George Washington would later call a "rising empire."[4]

Puritan violence, especially against the Indians, was the first American step in our long masculinized history of conquest. The Puritan attacks on Indians sickened Roger Williams, who founded Rhode Island partly due to his desire to develop a more humane relationship with the natives. Williams maintained masculinized ideals about religion, but his tilt toward feminized ideals of equality, toleration, and cooperation also led to his outrage at the Puritans' forced conversion of the Indians to Christianity. Williams described this form of masculinized coercion as one of "the most monstrous and most inhumane acts," and a "violation of Christian principles."[5]

The Puritans' values of expansion and violence lay at the heart of their masculinized economic dream. Puritans believed fervently in an individualistic "work ethic" and wealth accumulation. Hard work allowed each individual to prove to himself and others that he was among the saved. The Puritans' community was not a feminized community of equals, because some were predestined for Grace and others for Hell. The individualistic pursuit of wealth would distinguish the saved from the damned, and the masculinized pursuit of self-interest was elevated to godliness.[6]

This Puritan work ethic was a prime example of what sociologist Max Weber called the "Protestant ethic."[7] Weber argued that the Protestant Reformation and major Protestant sects, including the Calvinists and Puritans, created a new individualistic moral philosophy that gave rise to modern Western capitalism. In its emphasis on self-interest, competition, aggression, and personal wealth accumulation, Western capitalism was a robustly masculinized economic morality. In the United States, it helped create the most purely masculinized capitalist system in the world, a matter to which we return repeatedly.

The Founding Fathers created the United States about 150 years after the Puritan settlers arrived at Plymouth Rock. The fact that we call them "Fathers" symbolically affirms the masculinized identity of the new nation. But the first leaders of the country, while drawing on the legacy of the Puritans and the broader masculinized Anglo-American moral philosophy that they inherited, wrote some feminized values into the Declaration of

Independence and the Constitution. They created a masculinized nation with a subset of feminized ideals that the rising feminized majority can claim today as its own American heritage.

The Declaration of Independence was the most feminized creation of the Founding Fathers. Its ringing declaration that "all men are created equal" is, despite the masculinized language, a direct expression of feminized moral sensibility, because equality, as we show soon, is a centerpiece of feminized thinking. Moreover, the Declaration's focus on democracy and human rights, including the right to dissent and break away from a tyrant to form one's own self-government, is a foundational statement of American feminized values by the Founding Fathers.

But Jefferson, the author of the Declaration and the most feminized of the Founding Fathers, was simultaneously painting a broader masculinized picture that the Constitution would lock into place. Jefferson was schooled in the Anglo-American tradition of political morality shaped by the British philosopher John Locke. Locke's vision of rights grew out of a doctrinal concept of natural law that, as Harvard law professor Alan Dershowitz has shown, could become a form of dogma as rigid and masculinized as Puritan dogma.[8] Because natural law could not be proved or disproved, as it rested ultimately on religion and "reason" rather than empirical observation, it was an article of faith that the elites could interpret. The Founding Fathers found natural law consistent with the masculinized principles of slavery, disenfranchisement of women, and exclusionary property qualifications for the vote.

The Founders' moral vision became clearer in the Constitution, a far more masculinized doctrine than the Declaration of Independence. True, the Constitution had feminized values, reflected most strongly in the Bill of Rights and the Preamble, whose first words are "We, the People." The Preamble declares that the new self-governing community of the people is banding together to "form a more perfect Union," to "establish Justice," and to secure the "General Welfare." This expresses feminized values of democracy, community, social justice, and social welfare.

The Bill of Rights is the other most feminized element of the Constitution. Jefferson refused to sign on to the Constitution until his disciple, James Madison, the Constitution's principal author, added a bill of rights to the original text. Jefferson feared that the Constitution's vision of a strong centralized government could lead to a restoration of a British-style monarchy dressed up as a republic, a masculinized model of command authority that Alexander Hamilton, another chief author of the Constitution, found appealing. Jefferson believed that only the Bill of Rights could guarantee to the people the feminized values of that perfect Union, justice, and self-government that the Preamble had promised.

But Jefferson was deeply conflicted about matters ranging from slavery to national expansion to popular government, reflecting his uneasy, tortured blend of feminized and masculinized values. While the Bill of Rights may have reflected a feminized desire to protect "we the people" from centralized authority and tyranny, Jefferson drew from Locke a "negative" concept of rights built around the masculinized values of private property, individualism, and the right to be left alone.[9] This contrasted with a "positive" conception of rights to food, shelter, and a decent livelihood from the larger community or "perfect Union." This feminized vision of positive rights—based on values of equality, cooperation, and social welfare—found no home in the Bill of Rights or the broader Constitution.

The Founding Fathers viewed property as a central human right, a reflection of how deeply they were schooled in Locke's Anglo-American morality. Locke conceived private property as the ultimate guarantor of liberty. The Bill of Rights essentially assured that each man was the king of his own castle and safeguarded each individual's right to do with his wife, family, and land as he saw fit. To Locke, this was Natural Law; it was also a masculinized social construction that enshrined the moral narrative of *Alone I Will*. This masculinized vision of a fenced-off liberty clashes with the feminized model of freedom in community. The feminized communal view also competed with the individualistic, capitalistic model of private property that the first chief justice of the Supreme Court, John Marshall, fleshed out during his long tenure as the essence of the Constitution.[10]

The Constitution's equating of private property with liberty defined American capitalism as a masculinized project. But the Constitution was masculinized in other equally important ways. While upholding principles of resistance to traditional tyranny, the right to self-government, and the separation of powers—all consistent with a feminized sensibility as we show later—the Constitution promoted a restrictive vision of democracy that kept power in the hands of propertied male elites. This aversion to a more robust democratic vision reflected a masculinized hierarchic political morality and power system undergirding capitalism in the North and the slave system in the South.

The most obvious antidemocratic and masculinized elements of the Constitution involved denying citizenship to slaves and subordinating women. Counting slaves as a fraction of a person, who lacked any rights of citizenship and were the legal property of their male masters, is the most overtly antidemocratic aspect of the Constitution, essential to sustaining the hypermasculinized slave order of the South. The Founding Fathers made a Faustian bargain over race, accepting legalized slavery in southern states as a condition of the "perfect Union." The male masters of the South accepted the bargain because they could perpetuate their quasi-feudal power and economic plantation system in the name of the moral values of male protection, honor, and order. The male masters of the North saw this as a concession that would neither undermine profits nor threaten their vision of a republic guided by civilized white men.

The subordination of women was another overtly anti-democratic and masculinized element of the Constitution, serving the interests of male elites in both the South and North. As with slaves, this was rationalized within a masculinized moral and religious code. Men had the moral obligation to protect, honor, and guide women within a paternalistic vision of masculinized power that harkened back to the Puritans. This chivalrous patriarchy was especially highly developed in the South, where, as shown in the classic film *Gone with the Wind* (1939), romanticized medieval notions prevailed of a bucolic agrarian society with an aristocratic class of brave knights and landed gentry who protected beautiful and genteel women from the attacks of slaves or serfs.

A third antidemocratic and masculinized element of the Constitution was the harsh property qualifications for voting that limited the franchise mainly to affluent white men. The great American historian Charles Beard argued in his classic work, *An Economic Interpretation of the Constitution of the United States* (1913), that this gift of political influence to propertied classes animated the entire constitutional project.[11] Hamilton and other conservative Founders feared a roustabout populist democracy that would assert feminized values of equality and economic redistribution. Small farmers and craftsmen might demand cancellation of the debt that the new federal government owed its richest Revolutionary War creditors and benefactors. The Whiskey Rebellion and Shay's Rebellion, early populist uprisings by the propertyless, had made this threat real. The Constitution would seal off the prospects of a more egalitarian and social vision that the French revolutionaries of the era had pronounced with the feminized slogans of "Liberty, Equality, and Fraternity."

The constitutional "perfect Union" protected masculinized power and values against feminized populist and egalitarian sensibilities in other important ways. To secure the union with the South, the Founding Fathers set up the Senate, a profoundly undemocratic body that had no place in a democratic order. By awarding two senators to each state regardless of population, the Constitution gave male voters in relatively unpopulated southern and frontier states far more power than those in the more densely populated urban northern states. The same antidemocratic sensibilities led to the Electoral College and a multitiered system of representation, designed to remove decisionmakers from the popular vote and from direct accountability to ordinary citizens.[12]

Perhaps the most profound masculinized moral vision held by the Founding Fathers was the embrace of empire. James Madison expressed the Founders' view that the new republic could survive only by expanding and conquering more land, to avoid the "factionalism" and struggle over resources that would inevitably corrupt a small state. He wrote to Jefferson that a republic "must operate not within a small but extensive sphere," or as historian William Appleman Williams paraphrased him, "Empire was essential for freedom."[13] Nearly all the Founding Fathers, from Benjamin Franklin to John Adams and ultimately Jefferson himself, embraced this vision and explicitly conceived of America as destined by Providence to become a great empire.[14] While the more feminized Jefferson had qualms about this expansionist and ultimately militarized vision of America, when he became president he secured the Louisiana Purchase, which doubled the size of the country and represented the biggest land grab in American history. We return shortly to the Founders' masculinized view of empire and how it shaped a violent American history.

Jefferson's opening to the West symbolizes the enormous importance of the frontier in building an American masculinized morality. Frederick Jackson Turner was the most famous of many American historians to show how the frontier shaped American morals and character.[15] Most important for our story, the frontier entrenched masculinized values as the dominant mythology of an America on the move. The vast expanse of western land reinforced the mentality of an immigrant nation. Picking up and leaving was always an American path to freedom. The Puritan immigrants had taken this route, but they had done so as a community. The frontiersmen could pick up and move west on their own. This perfectly resonated with the master masculinized moral narrative: *Alone I Will*

The frontier beckoned individuals who dreamed of a future free of obligations, laws, and confining ties. It suited restless loners who believed in self-reliance and saw community as a shackle and government as a ball and chain. A Lockean paradise waited on the frontier, a world of one's own that could be fenced in, built with one's own sweat and blood, and defended with one's own gun. This frontier ethos took American masculinized values of individualism and elevated them to mythological status.

The frontier undermined community as a central American value, dealing a nearly fatal blow to an American feminized moral narrative.[16] American men, who had always been restless, mobile, and leery of commitment, could see endless freedom in the trek westward. The permanent open door of the frontier meant that community could never securely hold its more ambitious, adventuresome, discontented, or entrepreneurial men. The California gold rush epitomized the masculinized frontier morality that linked success to cutting loose and pursuing one's fortune on one's own.

The frontier reshaped the American Dream as radical individualism. It was each man for himself in the gold rush of the larger economy. Most men in the cities, of course, were chained to rising factories created by the new class of Gilded Age industrialists. But the frontier made credible the American Dream that every man could move on, find land, and build his own farm, business, and wealth relying only on himself.

The frontier was all about tough men who did what it took to survive. This represented frontier social Darwinism: the toughest, most resourceful, and best men would prevail. Hollywood immortalized these tough hombres in the westerns, making clear that the cowboys were not outlaws but men embodying a masculine morality of self-reliance, toughness, and the courage to fight to protect themselves and their families.[17]

The frontier elevated masculinized values consistent with the needs and ideology of the rough-and-tumble American capitalist order arising after the Civil War.[18] The Robber Barons who were building the railroads, the steel mills, and the oil plants—Jay Gould, John D. Rockefeller, Andrew Carnegie, and J. P. Morgan—were among the most masculinized capitalists in history: self-interested, aggressive, and often violent. They saw no limits to wealth on their own economic frontiers and ruthlessly used money and influence to build a capitalist order accommodating and moralizing their greed. They did not hesitate to use their own private police forces to crush worker revolts, calling in federal sheriffs or marshals when necessary, as in the infamous 1892 Homestead Mill steel strike where federal troops massacred striking workers. Andrew Carnegie, Homestead's owner and sheriff in charge, rejoiced when he heard from his chief officer on the scene, Henry Frick, that "we will not have any serious labor trouble again." Carnegie responded to Frick by telegram, "Congratulations ... life worth living again."[19] In 1890, when Rockefeller became the nation's first billionaire and 90 percent of Americans were poor, Rockefeller offered the morality of social Darwinism, tinged with Puritanism, to justify his wealth, claiming "God gave me my money."[20]

The Robber Barons brought a masculinized frontier morality into the heart of the capitalist world. Men would make it on their own without any limits placed on their ambition. The best and strongest would survive and prosper. Much of this was sheer myth, imported from the frontier, obscuring the intimate, collusive ties to the government that greased the rise of the new tycoons, ensuring them personal and systemic favoritism. Nonetheless, masculinized frontier values of self-interest, aggression, and violence became the moral building blocks of both the rising capitalist system and the ideology that made it appear sacred.[21]

The Gilded Age capitalism of the Robber Barons eventually gave way to a more refined, regulated system in the twentieth century. A new model arose that emphasized large-scale organization, management, high technology, and human capital. But the new system remained structurally and morally based on the masculinized values of self-interest, aggression, and survival of the fittest. The new organizational and managerial capitalism that came to rule modern America had a more rationalized veneer and incorporated women workers and managers as a new feminizing force, but it remained masculinized to its core. In later chapters, we bring this story of capitalism up to the present, and look closely at the challenges it now presents to the rising feminized majority.

Manifest Destiny, Conquest, and Empire

Males succeed in their corporate, military, and leadership roles by living out the values of aggression, violence, and conquest. When they are successful, they are affirmed as men, winning money, women, and medals. They also affirm the masculine identity of the United States as a nation. The masculinization of the United States is most vividly on display today in the war on terrorism, the huge, global presence of American bases and soldiers around the planet, and the overwhelming projection of power that makes America a twenty-first-century empire.

From the beginning, building America required aggression and violence. The land the settlers wanted was already occupied. Millions of Native Americans inhabited the "wilderness." Many tribes had highly developed cultures and social structures. Construction of the new nation destroyed them and their civilizations.

The very creation of the United States required men who would fight, armed with guns and a masculinized philosophy that could moralize violence and conquest. We need to return briefly here to the Puritans because they understood this and bred men and moral values that could do the job. John Winthrop's "shining city on the hill" served as the moral basis for a people that God had chosen to spread his influence across the continents, by words, deeds, and war when necessary.[22]

The brutality that led the early settlers to kill Indians who had helped them grow maize and survive the harsh winters reflected the masculinized morality of violence that became visible about the same time across the ocean in the martial Puritan rule of Cromwellian England. There, too, masculinized moral purity justified ruthless Puritan killing on a spectacular scale.[23] In the American context, the Puritans began the long project of forcibly displacing Indians from their land, and often killing them, as part of God's plan for his "shining city." As with Cromwell, ferocity melded with moral purity and idealism. In both cases, a masculinized morality redefined horrific violence as the conquest of savagery and the spread of virtue and civilization necessary to create God's kingdom on earth.

Each new generation of American settlers embraced their own story of the "shining city on the hill," providing a moral basis for the masculinized agenda of Empire. The "savages" were fought over and over to create an America from sea to shining sea, and it would take tough leaders with strong masculinized values to lead this noble charge. Even though the Founding Fathers intellectualized and partially feminized this imperial vision, being far less certain than the Puritans of God's sanction to slaughter the heathens, as introduced earlier, the Madisonian solution achieved the same larger aims of blessing American expansion and conquest. Madison's view that democracy required an expansive state to limit factionalism and a Hobbesian war for scarce resources provided an elegant secular argument for the conquest of Native American land, suggesting that the world's greatest democratic experiment depended on it—and that the Indians who cooperated would themselves benefit by being conquered and civilized.[24] As historian William Appleman Williams has shown in agonizing detail, virtually all the Founding Fathers signed on to this masculinized vision of a moral and democratic American empire.[25] In arguing for the Louisiana Purchase, Jefferson himself, the most feminized Founding Father and arguably founder of the Democratic Party, wrote that "the people of Louisiana were as yet incapable of self-government" and in 1809 proclaimed that "no constitution was ever before as well calculated as ours for extensive empires and self-government."[26] This argument linking empire and self-government resurfaced throughout American history from Teddy Roosevelt to Woodrow Wilson to George W. Bush.[27] Today's neoconservatives are the masculinized inheritors of this Madisonian and Jeffersonian legacy.

After the Founders, Andrew Jackson carried the masculinized values of war and conquest to the next level. This whiskey-drinking, Indian-killing, warrior president symbolized the masculinization of the United States in the nineteenth century. Jackson made no apology for his long project of removing the Indians from everywhere east of the Mississippi to secure more land for Southern slave plantations, telling Congress in 1833 that the Indians "must necessarily yield to the force of circumstances and ere long disappear."[28] But he justified his brutal military exploits with the masculinized moral ideals of the Puritans and the Founding Fathers, arguing that through American conquest and guidance the Indians would progress "from barbarism to the habits and enjoyments of civilized life."[29]

As Americans pushed Indians west of the Mississippi, the vast western frontier beckoned. Conquering the West was the final step necessary to create a continental United States—and launch new conquests across the Pacific, America's next steps toward a masculinized global empire. But since this grand national project necessitated not only removing and killing Indians, but also going to war against Mexico and Spain, it required an equally grand masculinized moral vision. The "shining city" evolved into a nineteenth-century grand doctrine of "Manifest Destiny," which would give moral sanction and God's blessing to a masculinized American empire of continental, and then global, scale.

Journalist and diplomat John L. Sullivan first introduced the phrase *Manifest Destiny* in 1839. He reframed the "shining city" as an American "Union of Republics," a great empire spanning the Atlantic to the Pacific. Manifest Destiny was the masculinized doctrine that became the moral foundation for U.S. foreign policy from the Mexican War to the War on Terror.[30]

Stephen Austin, who led Southern settlers invading Texas in Jackson's and Sullivan's era, was a masculinized warrior who ironically invoked Manifest Destiny and providential liberty to expand the slave empire of the South. In justifying war against Mexico to annex Texas, he wrote that "Texas was a wilderness ... the home of Comanches and other tribes of Indians." It was America's moral mission, Austin wrote, to "restrain these savages and bring them to subjection."[31] This was part of a larger argument for war against Mexico to promote the growing American empire's Manifest Destiny, which was in service of "the great cause of liberty, to ourselves, to our posterity, and to the free blood which I am proud to say, fills our veins."[32]

The history of America over the next fifty years was one of tough and brutal Indian fighters clearing the frontier for white settlers, ranchers, and gold rushers. General George Custer, Colonel John Shivington, and the like had what it took to get rid of the Indians and secure the rising American empire. As Custer, who said "the only good Indian is a dead Indian," and Shivington, who led the notorious 1864 Sand Creek Indian massacre in Colorado, and other supermasculinized fighters did this dirty work, American military heroes leading wars against Mexico and Spain became presidents, taking charge of the masculinized empire that America was becoming.

President Teddy Roosevelt, the swaggering "Rough Rider" who charged up the hill to help "liberate" Cuba from the evil Spaniards, symbolized the masculinized values America's new twentieth century empire demanded. Roosevelt, who had gone to the Dakota Badlands after college to ride horses and shoot guns, saw war as a masculine virtue and high moral calling. He called the Cuban intervention this "splendid little war" and wrote earlier, in 1895, that the "greatest boon" he could offer America was "an immediate war with Great Britain for the conquest of Canada."[33]

Roosevelt embodied some feminized values on the domestic front, encouraging conservation of the wilderness and forcing the hypermasculinized Robber Baron corporations to abide by progressive regulations that preserved but softened corporate power. But in foreign policy, he pursued an unabated masculinized expansionism, conceiving the United States in the twentieth century as a tough moral sheriff who would exercise "international police power." Having freed Cuba from the evils of Old World colonialism, he was eager to establish American domain over all Latin

America and across the Pacific, beginning with the colonization of the Philippines and then opening China and all Asia to American commerce and influence. But TR feared that the new twentieth-century American male might not be up to the task of this masculinized global challenge. After achieving the conquest of the West, American men were in danger of softening and becoming feminized. In 1907, when Harvard president Eliot proposed abolishing football at the college, Roosevelt countered: "We can not afford to turn out college men who shrink from physical effort or a little physical pain." America's new global empire needed masculinized men with "the courage that will fight valiantly against the foes of the soul and the foes of the body."[34] Roosevelt wanted to bring the masculinized identity bred on every boy's football field to the battlefields of the new global American empire.

Two world wars eventually destroyed the old European Empires and led America to global dominance. A half century after TR became president, his hypermasculinized dream of undisputed American "police power" would come true. As we discuss in a later chapter, Europe would feminize with the crumbling of its global empires after World War II, while America would become the world's hegemonic power and grab the masculinized mantle that hegemony brings. This masculinization of America intensified as the cold war heated up, and by the time Ronald Reagan vowed to destroy the Soviet "Evil Empire," masculinized morals and hormones were running wild in Washington and much of America. After the 9/11 attacks, George W. Bush would add more flames to this masculinized fire, as a macho American sheriff who fought evil while shouting, "Bring 'em on!" and "It's our way or the highway!" But Bush's vision of a hypermasculinized warrior America had to contend not only with a hostile and unreceptive world, but a rising feminized majority in the United States that had a different moral compass and vision of America.

CHAPTER THREE

The Rise of the Feminized Majority

Women are at the forefront of a values revolution in America that is moving the country away from its masculinized history into a new era of feminized progressivism. Although women are leading the charge, as the gender gap proves, many men are along for the ride. They, too, have grown tired of America's corporatist economic policies and cowboyesque foreign agenda. The growing number of women and men adopting feminized positions make up the new feminized majority with the potential to transform both the Democratic Party and the country.

In the next few chapters, we carefully examine the values and vision for America of the emerging feminized majority. In this chapter, we consider the historical and contemporary conditions giving rise to this new majority. We explore why it developed in the 1960s, continued to spread during the backlash of the Reagan revolution, and now may be reaching a tipping point, capable of moving the country in a decisive new direction from its masculinized past.

The 1960s, the 1980s Backlash,
and the Current Feminizing Forces

Women's values have become increasingly oppositional and are spreading rapidly. Women's increasing progressivism in polls is in stark contrast to their voting habits during the 1950s. Harvard researcher Pippa Norris examines these differences:

> *The American Voter* (Campbell et al. 1960) found that in presidential elections from 1952 to 1960 women were slightly more Republican than men, with a gender gap in the region of 3–5 percent. In the 1956 midterm elections, for example, men voted decisively (58 percent) in favor of the Democrats while women gave the edge to the Republicans (52 percent). The pattern in NES data was confirmed by Gallup polls, which registered stronger female support for the Republican Presidential candidate in every election during the 1950s.[1]

The 1950s were the final years of the old paradigm. Women, who had gotten the vote only a few decades earlier, voted less in line with feminized values, responding to the avuncular style of General (and then president) Eisenhower, who offered a reassuring version of the traditional masculinized model of leadership and male protection. Women were socialized to accept a subordinate role in the 1950s patriarchal order and voted accordingly.

The 1960s led to a sea change in political opinions and set into motion a long-term values revolution against the masculinized American order. Beyond the tendency for women to act and vote independently rather than compliantly follow their husbands and male leaders, two structural factors in the 1960s created an atmosphere conducive to feminized social change: (1) Rising and pervasive economic inequality caused many Americans to rethink masculinized capitalist ideals, and (2) the Vietnam War led many Americans to question the masculinized virtues of war.

These structural conditions produced some of the most dramatic social movements in American history, including the civil rights movement, the antiwar movement, a student movement for participatory economic democracy, and a second-wave feminist movement. They collectively challenged the entire system of American masculinized power. While some were short lived, all were revolutionary forces that changed the country and gave birth to the feminized majority.

Two elements of the 1960s movements deserve attention. First, they were fundamentally moral in nature. In his famous "I Have a Dream" speech in 1963, Martin Luther King Jr., a preacher and inspiration for all the sixties movements, laid out a new moral vision for America. King challenged not only the values underlying racial segregation and the Vietnam War, but those undergirding the American political economy. His challenge to the traditional, individualized sink-or-swim American Dream was taken as a guiding manifesto by all the 1960s movements. King spearheaded one of the most radical moral revolutions in American history.

Second, these movements reflected the expression of a feminized values revolt. The new feminists created the only movement of the era to explicitly cast their cause as a feminizing revolution against a masculinized order. The other movements were asserting the core feminized values of equality, community, and peace, though they didn't define themselves as feminist. The fights against racial segregation, corporate capitalism, and the Vietnam War were different expressions of a feminized moral sensibility just beginning to assert itself against 200 years of American masculinized hegemony. They spread the soil in which the new feminized majority would germinate and flower, long after the decline of the sixties itself.

Because the 1960s constituted such a profound moral revolution, it inevitably bred a ferocious moral backlash. Mobilized in the cultural arena by Christian conservatives and in the economic arena by corporate elites, a Republican New Right successfully organized to reassert traditional masculinized moral values. In the name of family values, religion, and economic freedom, the New Right succeeded, in 1980, in electing Ronald Reagan and instituting a new masculinized era.

The Reagan revolution was itself fundamentally moral, a politically orchestrated effort to delegitimize the 1960s revolt as un-American, communist, and morally degenerate. At the level of national politics and mass media, the backlash achieved striking success. As the sixties receded, the sixties movements were redefined as the creation of spoiled affluent kids whose only morality was hedonistic self-indulgence. The view of the 1960s as morally transformative and emancipatory became almost laughable among elites, who shared and propagated the alternative view of a 1960s era that destroyed any moral values worth preserving.

But while the elite backlash was taking hold, it failed to stop the quiet growth of the new values that the sixties movements had seeded. In the next chapter, we report empirical data that show how feminized values continued to spread even as conservative Republicans took center stage in Washington. Although they had no political vehicle for expression of these values at the national level, ordinary Americans became increasingly feminized in their values, lifestyles, and social philosophy. A new moral majority was quietly being born.

As we now move through the third decade of the Reagan-inspired backlash, new challenges are giving this "silent majority" a sense of urgency. Disparities in wages between top-level executives and average workers are increasing at astonishing rates. Free trade agreements, corporate mergers, and white-collar crime are creating an atmosphere of job insecurity and financial worry for everyday citizens. The war in Iraq has become a quagmire. America's character is being questioned by the entire world due to the military's practices at Abu Ghraib and Guantanamo Bay. And in an era of illegal wiretaps, the PATRIOT Act, and imprisonment without charge or trial, even many Americans are wondering what their country is really all about.

Women face unique challenges in this environment. More and more, women are being pulled in many directions at once. A woman is expected to work full time *and* be the primary caregiver to her children. Many women are their children's sole caregiver. It is perhaps unsurprising, then, that women at all socioeconomic levels are seeking changes to America's masculinized economic system. The social Darwinism of unrestrained capitalism does not appeal to women, who are usually the ones responsible for ensuring that their children are fed and clothed. Further, women now seek an end to hypermasculinized foreign policy. The protection promised with the war in Iraq—which many pundits allege was rooted in the "security mom" phenomenon—has actually created *more* terrorists.[2] Beyond issues of safety, women are sensitive to global humanitarian issues, perhaps because they are responsible for explaining their country's actions to their children. When children see hooded prisoners with electrodes attached to their bodies, women are put in the unenviable position of either convincing the children that torture is sometimes justifiable or that their country is wrong.

Although women are in a unique position as workers and mothers, times are also particularly hard for the many men who are realizing that the values they carry and cherish no longer seem to fit reality. Many men are unable to provide for their families or to protect them from economic hardship. The self-defense tactics they learned as children on the playground are not working for their country in the global war on terror. It is a confusing time to be an American man.

Other forces are contributing to the rapid ascension of the feminized base. The thirst for change, started in the 1960s but repressed by corporate politicians for two decades after Reagan's election, is now back with new fervor. We consider, first, the "corporatization of America" and its bitter fruits and, second, military failures and the decline of America's global hegemony—two factors that are delegitimizing ruling masculinized values and spreading feminized values across the land.

Corporatization and Economic Insecurity

In 1964 President Johnson announced in his State of the Union address that his administration was pursuing a "War on Poverty." He lamented that "many Americans live on the outskirts of hope—some because of their poverty, and some because of their color, and all too many because of both. Our task is to help replace their despair with opportunity."[3] Johnson called on Congress to embrace the values of community and empathy. To win this "war," he proposed a number of feminized programs as part of a "cooperative approach."[4] He pushed federal, state, and local governments to work together. His call to action was the start of a much larger effort. Building on the progress made by Roosevelt's New Deal programs, the Johnson administration created Job Corps, Head Start, and VISTA. In the decade after the programs' inception, the poverty rate hit a low of 11.1 percent.[5] It has not been that low since.

The Johnson era struck fear in the hearts of many conservatives. In the 1970s, a masculinized backlash began against the social programs created by FDR and Johnson. The 1980 election of Ronald Reagan led to the reversal of many feminized policies and ushered in an era of globalized corporatism. The trend continued in the 1990s, with Bill Clinton proudly explaining in a debate against Bob Dole that his administration had "reduced the size of the federal government to its smallest size in 30 years."[6] Many poverty experts consider Clinton's welfare reform legislation of 1996 emblematic of the backlash against social programs. If anything, welfare reform certainly proved that a masculinized view of poverty was bipartisan among elites.

In the twenty-first century, we are finally seeing the full effects of corporatist economic policies: The divide between the rich and the poor is the largest since the Gilded Age, American CEOs have individual incomes that rival the gross domestic products (GDPs) of many countries, and elections are almost entirely funded by corporations and the wealthy. Since the 1970s, the income of the top quintile of Americans has gone up 63 percent. The income of the poorest 20 percent of Americans rose by 2 percent.[7] "It's not that the poor are getting poorer," writes journalist Matt Bai, "or that more poor Americans are falling below the poverty line, so much as it is that poor Americans are falling further and further behind those who succeed."[8] While more and more Americans are struggling to get by, other Americans are doing astonishingly well. The *Forbes Magazine* list of the 400 wealthiest Americans is almost entirely made up of billionaires.[9]

In the face of this bleak economic picture, a new feminized populism has emerged. The 1980s destroyed many of the gains made by feminized values in the 1960s. However, during this decade the gender gap emerged as a political phenomenon. The procorporate economic policies of Ronald Reagan motivated many insecure voters—the majority of whom were women—to doubt the economy's fairness and the masculinized system of dog-eat-dog capitalism. The 1990s, with countless corporate mergers and downsizings, led both female and male voters to seek changes in the relationship between politics and business. And, in the twenty-first century, a new sense of urgency has developed.

Growing inequality is a serious threat to America's culture, which is built upon the idea that anyone can make it. In gendered terms, the failure of this promise strikes a serious blow to masculinized, individualized values.

Working-class women and men are falling behind, and it will take more than them pulling themselves up by their bootstraps to help them. These workers show that, in today's society, the American Dream is a myth. They work hard to uphold their end of the "bargain," only to learn that their job has been outsourced or that their wages are inadequate to pay for food *and* rent. From a masculinized values perspective, these workers are failures. They did not work hard enough, or they just lack the skills to succeed. If a worker is a man, he failed twice, because he could not provide for his family and he did not live up to masculinized values.

As more Americans now work long hours and still face stagnant incomes and more insecurity, millions have begun to question whether the economic order really works for them. As we show in polling data documented in the next chapter, a large majority of Americans express anger at global corporations and CEOs. As more workers continue to fall through the cracks, faith in the masculinized corporate system is eroding. This crumbling of masculinized values will ultimately increase the political strength of feminized values and the new feminized majority. Those Democrats who deny the new inequality by embracing masculinized corporations impair the ability of the feminized majority to assert itself sooner. It may take time until the Democratic Party explicitly addresses inequality and the masculinized corporate culture that is producing it. But the harsh effects of globalization and corporate power will continue to seed feminized values and fuel populist anger.

Failed Wars, Declining Hegemony, and Feminization

The 1960s also contributed to the rise of the feminized base with the birth of the modern antiwar movement.

The failure of the Vietnam War planted new doubts in the minds of many voters and led them to seek policy changes in U.S. international relations. Many Americans angrily rejected the idea that violence is a necessary step in attaining global peace. Although the Reagan era backlash slowed the growth of this feminized foreign policy consciousness, the Iraq War has given feminized voters a new sense of urgency.

The power of the United States emerged under a system of hegemonic capitalism. Hegemony involves nothing more than dominance, competition, and control; hegemonic capitalism relies on forcing open new markets to spread U. S. commerce.[10] Since the values of hegemony are masculinized values, we can see how hegemony can be viewed as a gendered term and how failure and decline in U.S. global hegemony are spurring growth of the new feminized majority.

In *Of Paradise and Power: America and Europe in the New World Order* (2003), Robert Kagan examines the relationship of hegemony and values. Kagan was a founding member of the Project for a New American Century, a neoconservative think tank that aims to spread peace and democracy around the world through U.S.-led regime change. Kagan also worked at the State Department, but now lives in Brussels with his wife and two children. Using the United States and Europe as representations of powerful and weak states, Kagan shows how a nation (or group of nations) reacts to world events differently based on its capabilities.

Perhaps living in Europe fueled Kagan's curiosity about what causes the United States and Europe to disagree so strongly about issues of international relations. He begins provocatively: "It is time to stop pretending that Europeans and Americans share a common view of the world, or even that they occupy the same world." As he shows, Europeans view the United States as has having a very different "strategic culture" than theirs:

The United States, they argue, resorts to force more quickly and, compared with Europe, is less patient with diplomacy. Americans generally see the world divided between good and evil, between friends and enemies, while Europeans see a more complex picture. When confronting real or potential adversaries, Americans generally favor policies of coercion rather than persuasion, emphasizing punitive sanctions over inducements to better behavior, the stick over the carrot.[11]

Europe's view of its own citizens is very different:

[Europeans] try to influence others through subtlety and indirection. They are more tolerant of failure, more patient when solutions don't come quickly. They generally favor peaceful responses to problems, preferring negotiation, diplomacy, and persuasion to coercion. They are quicker to appeal to international law, international conventions, and international opinion to adjudicate disputes. They try to use commercial and economic ties to bind nations together.[12]

Most interesting about Kagan's analysis of the United States and Europe is the metaphor he chooses to describe why these two powers do not see eye to eye. "On major strategic and international questions today," Kagan writes, "*Americans are from Mars, and Europeans are from Venus: They agree on little and understand one another less and less.*"[13]

Without explicitly saying so, Kagan has genderized the United States and Europe. The word "United States" is code for "power" and "Europe" for "weakness." And if power is from Mars, and weakness from Venus, Kagan's work implicitly acknowledges gendered values. Kagan nuances his argument by describing some Americans as more "European" than others. He writes, "In the United States, Democrats often seem more 'European' than Republicans; Secretary of State Colin Powell may seem more 'European' than Secretary of Defense Donald Rumsfeld."[14]

It's not much of a stretch to replace Kagan's choice of the word "European" with the word "feminized."

The strength of the United States and weakness of Europe, Kagan argues, lead them to care about and value different things. Kagan paraphrases a European political writer. Again, notice the gendered undertones of this assessment of American and European concerns:

> According to one student of European opinion, even the very focus on "threats" differentiates American policymakers from their European counterparts. Americans, writes Steven Everts, talk about foreign "threats" such as "the proliferation of weapons of mass destruction, terrorism, and 'rogue states.'" But Europeans look at "challenges," such as "ethnic conflict, migration, organized crime, poverty, and environmental degradation."[15]

The United States maintains its position of masculinized dominance not just by *having* a large military, but also by using it. Most Americans remember the United Nations Security Council meetings before the Iraq War, and French president Jacques Chirac's threat to veto any resolution giving the United States permission to invade Iraq. France, as a European (or feminized) nation, preferred to exhaust all diplomatic outlets before considering the option of force. Kagan would understand why France chose a different approach. "Those with great military power," Kagan writes, "are more likely to consider force a useful tool of international relations than those who have less military power."[16] In other words, military dominance both reflects and reinforces masculinized values of aggression and violence, while military weakness promotes feminized values of diplomacy and international law.

What is important about Kagan's argument is that the relative positions of the United States and Europe are new. Europe did not used to be feminized. At one time, the empires of Europe enjoyed the kind of global dominance that gave masculinized values of military aggression and force credibility among European publics. When European nations lost their hegemony (or masculinized control), their values started to change. Kagan points to the period between World War I and World War II as the first time that Europe tried to move beyond "power politics" and "make a virtue out of weakness." Europe created the idea of "collective security" and began experimenting with international institutions. When the European empires collapsed after World War II, European nations underwent a moral transformation and became increasingly feminized, repudiating the masculinized, hegemonic values that led the continent into two catastrophic world wars.

U.S. Hegemonic Decline and the Feminization of America

As progressives, we disagree with much of Kagan's approach, including his defense of U.S. global hegemony as both moral and necessary. He also fails to understand that American hegemony is beginning to erode. But his analysis is useful for understanding gendered politics; it implicitly suggests that hegemony is gendered. Masculinized, patriarchal values help foster the drive toward hegemony. Nations in a structural position of hegemony tend to promote and reinforce a masculinized moral view among their own citizens, which drapes the corporate interests fueling hegemony in a deeply resonating moral philosophy of freedom and prosperity. When hegemonic nations decline, and this moral perspective no longer makes sense to ordinary citizens as wars bleed the country and their own children, it opens up a window for the rise and spread of new feminized values, a process we believe could reshape America.

After World War II, with Europe in bloody tatters, the United States was left standing as the most powerful nation in the world. The American economy generated about 50 percent of the world's total manufacturing production.[17] The U.S. military deployed awesome strike forces on bases all over the world, displaying a capability and willingness to dominate governments on all continents. The Soviet Union, while an ideological foe, had seen more than 60 million of its people killed in the two world wars. It had neither the economic nor military muscle to serve as an effective counterweight to the new American hegemon.

Along with a growing number of analysts, we believe that although the United States remains the world's most powerful nation, it is experiencing an uneven and fitful slide toward hegemonic decline.[18] The decline, both economic and military, is creating a crisis of world order and a crisis of confidence in America itself. We believe that this crisis goes beyond the collapse of public support for the Bush administration. It is a deeper crisis of values. The new feminized majority reflects the erosion of masculinized values that American hegemony bred and the spread of feminized values that make more sense to Americans as their government's global economic and military policy seems increasingly suicidal.

Hegemony is always rooted in economic strength, which requires and makes possible ever more military interventionism. While the United States remains the world's largest economy, its share of the global economic pie has shrunk dramatically from 50 percent to less than 25 percent.[19] Partly through early American help in the 1950s Marshall Plan, the European nations, integrated into the European Union, are now collectively a larger economic force than the United States. And globalization is helping India, China, and other rising powers in Asia to become serious rivals to American economic hegemony.

The harsh U.S. corporate policies we described earlier are sapping the long-term strength of the American economy. Global giants like Exxon, GE, and Lockheed Martin may be enjoying huge short-term profits, but

American workers face losses in education, health care, and security that have sustained them as the world's most productive workforce. As this feminizes a workforce that no longer experiences the benefits from U.S. capitalist policies, it also undermines the foundations for American hegemony.[20] Also contributing to the decline of U.S. economic dominance was its increasing military expenditures, diverting capital from the nondefense sector as the East Asian economies and Europe were keeping military expenditures low and experiencing high investment and growth in their nondefense civilian economic sectors.[21]

Instead of demilitarizing after World War II, the United States used the cold war against the Soviets as a basis for expanding its global military force and overthrowing governments in one regime change after another on every continent. But its massive, failed intervention in Vietnam signaled the limits of American global power.[22] The Vietnam War caused an economic crisis in the United States, creating huge deficits and forcing it off the gold standard. It also created massive political resistance internationally and among America's own citizens. Social movements in the sixties challenged the moral legitimacy of American hegemony and American values. The "Vietnam Syndrome"—a new wave of moral revulsion against the imperial use of American military power and against the morality of violence itself—was an early signal of American hegemonic crisis amidst the rise and spread of feminized values.[23]

The loss and moral crisis of Vietnam did not end American hegemony, as U.S. corporations were just gearing up to exploit the enormous profits offered by a globalized marketplace. To secure those distant but lucrative markets, military forces were more necessary than ever, and the corporate regime under Ronald Reagan made sure they were available. While the Republicans led the hegemonic revival after Vietnam, the Clintons and the

Democratic Party supported the basic policy. After 9/11, George W. Bush pushed the hegemonic policy to its ultimate limits by launching preemptively the Iraq War and enshrining the "War on Terror" that was, as journalist Seymour Hersh dubbed it, America's "ticket to ride" anywhere in the world.

The result has been catastrophic for the world and America itself, creating a tipping point in U.S. hegemony. The arrogance and brutality of U.S. power, although couched in the lofty rhetoric of spreading democracy, created a massive global backlash, with the United States increasingly unpopular and seen as the greatest threat to world peace. Inside the United States itself, as the Iraq War bled the U.S. treasury, the population realized that imperial foreign adventures were preventing the country from providing its own citizens good education, quality health care, or even military security itself. Because a hegemon cannot long survive without the moral support of its own people, public revulsion with the Bush administration has begun to create a serious and enduring challenge to U.S. hegemony itself.[24]

The sight of U.S. soldiers demolishing Iraqi homes and killing thousands of Iraqi civilians—while thousands of GIs are themselves killed by roadside bombs in the nightmarish mayhem of the Iraqi occupation and civil war—has created a profound moral challenge to the masculinized values of aggression, violence, and domination that underpin hegemony. The Vietnam Syndrome will look small compared to the political and moral consequences of the Iraq catastrophe. As its military forces suffer the "overstretch" that led to the collapse of earlier great powers, America's own economic, social, and environmental fabric is stretched and torn to the breaking point. The symbol of New Orleans after Hurricane Katrina has become an iconic image for what is happening to America after Iraq and the endless War on Terror—a society unable to keep its own great cities from drowning.

This social drama in the United States is far from the wholesale, precipitous collapse of Europe after World War II, but it creates a similar deep crisis in values. As a large majority of Americans consistently tell pollsters that their country is going "in the wrong direction," they are struggling to find a new moral compass as masculinized, hegemonic values have failed them. The overwhelming need to rebuild America together, and to create a more peaceful world in concert with other nations, are the pillars of the feminized master narrative of *Together We Can*. Feminized values of cooperation, mutual caretaking, and local and global community through law and diplomacy become compelling in the wake of mayhem brought on by the masculinized values of individualism, competition, violence, and dominance.

The question is: Will this lead to a sea change in values in the United States, as such hegemonic failures did in Europe? As gender gap research shows, the United States *has* started changing. The 1960s, with the failure of the Vietnam War, led many Americans to reexamine what role America should play in the global community. Although Reagan created a backlash against this feminized movement, his actions were not a total reversal of the feminized values revolution started in the 1960s. Hegemonic declines tend to go in fitful cycles. So, too, does the decline of hegemonic, masculinized values. The elections of Reagan and Bush represent conservatives' attempts to fend off the inevitable values revolution that has yet to come to fruition.

Social Movements and the Feminization of America

The failures of corporatism and decline of hegemony are shaking the American system. As profound as these economic and military factors are, structural forces alone are not enough to create a revolution of values. It takes the collective power of average citizens to change the culture and reform a nation. While structural conditions provide the environment for change to occur, it is ultimately social movements, made up of ordinary citizens struggling to find a new moral compass, that catalyze values revolutions and force political parties to act on those values.

Germany offers an interesting example of how the values of a nation can change when its citizens engage in self-reflection. After World War II, the younger generation had to confront the catastrophe created by the values and politics of their parents. When one of us (Derber) went to Germany a few years ago, he asked many people he met about how Germany had changed so deeply. Compared to the Hitler era, Germany seemed like a far softer and gentler country now, indeed, more feminized.

Germans indicated that the younger generation after the war engaged in a painful rethinking of everything: their families, philosophies, and politics; their speech, expressions, and relationships; the morality of their country; and their own values. Many described a lifetime of questioning, which was passed on to a second generation after the war. It led ultimately to new women's, peace, and environmental movements, as well as new important political parties, such as the Green Party, and a change in the philosophy of the parties away from the authoritarian approaches on both the Communist Left and, especially, the Fascist Right.

In the United States, the inequality and violence of the 1960s provoked many citizens also to fight for a different future. The rise of new social movements during this time created an era of hope from what had been an age of despair about segregation and the Vietnam War. Passionate and persistent activists forced those in power to recognize that the old values driving political decisions no longer fit reality. The civil rights movement, second-wave feminism, and the antiwar movement presented a new kind of America, based on the values of peace, equality, and community. Although each movement had different leaders, tactics, and objectives, they were similar in the way they challenged the basic moral structure of a capitalist and hegemonic America. The seeds of a new moral philosophy, expressing the feminized master narrative of *Together We Can*, were planted during this time.

Women in this era went through a unique transformation. As we showed, women in the 1950s tended to vote Republican slightly more than men. The 1960s and its social movements changed the political landscape dramatically. Women, who once voted with their husbands, began to see themselves as independent and autonomous, with the right to sovereignty over themselves and their vote choices.[25] Inspired by the civil rights movement, and emboldened by feminism, women began looking at the world—and their place in it—in a whole new way. In the years since, women began deviating from men in their vote choices and began expressing feminized values in new and more autonomous ways. Now, as we know, the majorities of women and men in the electorate consistently vote for different presidents while thinking differently across the whole gamut of political issues.

In the years following the rise of new social movements, a backlash emerged, epitomized by the election of Ronald Reagan. Years of rumbling hostility toward the new values of the 1960s came to the surface, and social movements were repressed and weakened. The era of Reagan was a dark time for progressive activists, as corporations became enmeshed with partisan politics, and social puritans and military hawks became the leaders of America.[26]

Unfortunately for conservatives, feminized values had already become deeply rooted, and were spreading far beyond the membership of the social movements. In the decades of corporate backlash, when social movements waxed and waned in an oppressive atmosphere, feminized values in the population continued to strengthen and evolve. As much as conservatives attempted to reverse the progress made by social movements, and as much as they succeeded in silencing the movements themselves, the new values planted by social movements stuck. In fact, polls show that Americans continued to become more feminized as the corporate backlash continued.[27]

Still, the Reagan era shows how an unfriendly political atmosphere can hinder social movements. And unfortunately for progressive activists, the United States lacks a mainstream political party that nurtures social movements. The Democratic Party has moved away from activists in the past thirty years in favor of more centrist and corporatist ideals, as evidenced by the dismal showing of Democratic congresspersons at national antiwar protests or gay and lesbian rights rallies. Social movements now have few steadfast allies in Washington.

The current condition of the Democratic Party makes the work of social activists even more important in America; activists must provide the voice that is suppressed by both major parties. Whether or not political parties admit it, a majority of Americans want dramatic changes in this country. And polls show that these changes are rooted in feminized values. Like a crop that grows after a long drought, feminized values are underground no more. The Democratic Party can either become a part of this new movement, or it can get left behind.

Chapter Four

Women's Values
and a New America

The rising feminized majority has a different vision of America, but what is this vision and how widespread is it? In this chapter, we examine polling data about public opinion to answer these questions. In the first part, we present gender gap research concerning women's values and vision for America. It's a story about a desire for a new America, far more progressive than that currently embraced by the Democratic Party. In the second part, we prove that a robust majority of Americans already share a feminized vision for major social change. That will happen only if the Democratic Party seizes the opportunity.

Gender gap research documents our argument that: (1) men and women have different values, (2) these differing values spill over into the political arena, and (3) women's values lead to a progressive vision for economic and social transformation in America. Gender gap research also highlights how millions of men share feminized values and a progressive vision for the country. Then, we show that extensive polling research documents that the feminized majority's views resonate with a majority of American voters. In the next chapter, we spell out more clearly why these progressive values are feminized and how "feminized" politics differ from both feminism and traditional liberalism or progressivism.

The Gender Gap

Substantial research suggests that gendered values affect the private and public decisions of men and women. This research focuses on the political "gender gap" that emerged in the mid-1980s, a phenomenon proving that men and women do not see eye to eye on many issues. The term *gender gap* initially measured the difference in the number of men and women who vote for a specific political candidate. In the 1996 presidential election, for example, a 12 percentage-point gap separated the number of women who supported Bill Clinton and the number of men who supported Bill Clinton.

The gender gap also refers to the difference in the number of men and women who support a certain position on a political issue. For example, a 2007 Harris poll found a large gender gap between the number of women and men who oppose "Don't Ask, Don't Tell" military policy. Sixty-one percent of women want the policy overturned, compared to 47 percent of men—a 14 percentage-point gender gap.[1]

Today, few people doubt either the existence or the political importance of a large gender gap. In the last three elections, a majority of female voters *and* male voters supported different presidential candidates. In 2004, 51 percent of women voted for John Kerry, compared to just 44 percent of men.[2] In 2000, 54 percent of women voted for Al Gore, compared to 42 percent of men.[3] In 1996, as we noted, Bill Clinton was reelected with a large gender gap.

The 1990s is significant not only for the increasing size of the gender gap, but also because, for the first time, men and women actually voted in opposite directions.[4] In the 1980s, by contrast, a majority of both men and women voted for Reagan. In 1980, men voted for Reagan by an 18 percent margin while women voted for him by a 2 percent margin.[5]

A September 2007 poll suggested that the gender gap is growing dramatically. It showed that 53 percent of women planned to vote Democratic for president in 2008 compared to 27 percent who planned to vote Republican. Only 41 percent of men in the same poll said they would vote Democratic for president, while 37 percent said they would vote for the Republican presidential candidate.[6]

Gender gap data show that women of all demographic groups are trending more Democratic. Even among traditionally more conservative women—those married and living in suburbs—a plurality of 46 percent said they planned to vote Democratic for president in 2008 compared to only 29 percent who said they would vote Republican. In contrast, in 2004, while 51 percent of women voted for Kerry, married women voted 55 percent for Bush and 44 percent for Kerry, compared to single women who voted 62 percent for Kerry and only 37 percent for Bush.[7]

Because of their underlying values, women not only *vote* more liberally but also hold more *progressive views* than men on most political issues. Women are more likely than men to support civil unions for same-sex couples, and less likely to say that homosexuality is a choice.[8] They are more opposed to the death penalty, especially for minors.[9] They are more likely to support a pullout date for the troops in Iraq.[10] These opinions put women further to the left on the ideological spectrum than most men, and much further to the left than most evangelicals.

At the same time, women, perhaps unexpectedly, are *more* religious than men. Eighty-three percent of women over fifty, and 65 percent of women under fifty, rate religion as "extremely important," compared to 59 percent of men over fifty and 56 percent of men under fifty.[11] Women also are more likely than men (by a 37 percent to 29 percent margin) to believe that the Bible should have greater influence over American law than the will of the people.[12] How is it possible that women are both more religious than men and more progressive?

Women are still socialized to move through life with the goal of *Together We Can.* Women's gendered values encourage them to view issues differently than men, even if they share the same level of religiosity as men. Researcher Karen Kaufmann observes, "Men who believe that new lifestyles are bad and that new moral values should not be tolerated are more likely to be conservative on social welfare issues than women who hold similar beliefs."[13] Women with traditional moral values are more progressive than men with traditional moral values because they look at the same issues in different ways. In the case of social welfare, religious women share with other women the feminized values of community and equality and are more supportive of social programs, while traditionally religious men disapprove of welfare because they hold the masculinized values of individualism and competition. When traditional moral values intersect with feminized or masculinized values, it does not lead to the same conclusion. And, more generally, *when feminized values are applied to politics, they translate into a more progressive politics.*

Values emerge again and again as the reason women and men hold different political opinions. One study attributed political gender gaps to women's "egalitarian values" and their desire to "help others."[14] These traits make women more likely than men to support racial and gender equality. Women are also more likely to agree with the idea that the government should have more responsibility in helping its citizens and that government is better able to handle problems than is the free market. Not surprisingly, these values make women more likely to consider themselves liberal. Egalitarian values remain statistically significant even when controlling for income, education, occupational status, and religiosity.[15]

Men's views about the role of government in citizens' lives differ from women's views. Men are more likely to prefer a free market approach to social problems. In this sense, men's values closely align with capitalist values. Traditional capitalism was built on the values of competition, winner-take-all individualism, and inequality. The masculinized value system also includes individualism and competition—men are socialized to believe that *Alone I Will*. As government programs and a strong social welfare state restrain capitalism, they also end up at odds with masculinized values. More men than women, for example, feel that the government is "wasteful and inefficient," and would prefer a smaller government with fewer services to a larger government with more services.[16]

It seems historically appropriate that masculinized values are closely intertwined with capitalist values. Men were traditionally socialized to believe that, with hard work, they could move up the socioeconomic ladder. They were encouraged to use capitalism to pursue their dreams. Women, on the other hand, were traditionally socialized to take care of the home, providing unpaid domestic labor that has little value in a capitalist economy. Historically, women have not had the same relationship with capitalism as men, so their values intersect with capitalism in different ways than men's values. In fact, feminized values often counter capitalist values—cooperation versus competitiveness, for example. Social programs and other liberal approaches fit into the feminized value system, whereas they encroach on the masculinized value system.

Women and men also have strikingly different opinions regarding security and force. These differences were highlighted on 12 September 2001—the day after the attacks on the World Trade Center and the Pentagon—when a *CBS News* poll asked if respondents felt that the "U.S. should take military action against whoever is responsible for the attacks, even if it means that innocent people are killed." A full 75 percent of men agreed that the United States should take action, compared to 57 percent of women—an 18 percentage-point gender gap.[17]

This and other polls suggest that women think about war in a very distinct way. Because women value negotiation and cooperation over force—partly reflecting the historical reality that women have been victims of so much violence and women's caretaking roles in the family—they are more likely than men to renounce violence in all spheres of life. In politics, they are much more hesitant to support violent intervention to solve international conflicts. The gender gap in the 1980 election between Carter and Reagan highlights women's reluctance to support hawkish candidates. By controlling for concerns about armed conflict, researchers found that the gender gap disappeared.[18]

Not only are women less likely to support war as a tool to attain peace, they also have different feelings from men about acceptable codes of conduct during war. An *ABC News* poll found that 44 percent of men think that torture is acceptable in some circumstances, compared to only 27 percent of women. Fifty-four percent of men, compared with 39 percent of women, believe that physical abuse that stops short of torture is sometimes acceptable.[19] The issue of holding prisoners at Guantanamo Bay without filing formal charges against them divides men and women. Men support the government's policies at Guantanamo Bay by a 52 percent to 40 percent margin, while women oppose it 46 percent to 37 percent.[20] Perhaps women's feelings about Guantanamo come from their attitudes about equality under the law, the inherent humanity of all people, or sympathy for the families of those being detained. Any of these explanations are part of a feminized value system.

Toward a Feminized Majority

Gender gap data show that women are leading the way toward a more progressive politics. But they are doing more than that. They are actually creating a nation that is in line with their values: a feminized America. However, we should not assume that these trends point to a forthcoming battle-of-the-sexes ideological showdown. As more women vote in line with a feminized worldview, more men are actually *joining* them.

Feminized values are becoming majoritarian values. Bill Clinton, for example, was reelected with 43 percent of the male vote.[21] Because a large enough majority of women supported Clinton, the progressive choice for president became the majoritarian choice. The same can be true for political issues. Men are more likely to have conservative positions on political issues, but the majoritarian view can still be progressive, as more women vote and more men hold feminized values.

As we mentioned in the Introduction, our portrayal of Americans as feminized may seem counterintuitive in a time of terrorist threats, bans on same-sex marriage, and attacks on a woman's right to choose. The global community certainly doesn't see America as having become more progressive in the past decade. If anything, the reelection of George W. Bush in 2004 showed the world that the United States is on a fast track to right-wing territory uncharted in our nation's history. Moreover, many Americans find it hard to believe that there is a progressive majority in their own country. However, countless polls from the most reputable surveying agencies prove that, despite an influential conservative minority, the majority is, in fact, more progressive than ever before. And, as we discuss more fully in Chapter 5, this majority is feminized not because women are disproportionately represented but because women's values give rise to their progressive vision. This is not an interest-driven majority—seeking to advance the narrower interests of racial minorities, the working class, or even women themselves—but a morally driven community seeking to nurture the entire society in the spirit of the feminized values we have already identified.

Many advocacy organizations are catching onto the idea that Americans are far more progressive than conventional political wisdom would have us think. We draw on scores of national polls in this section. We also rely on several reports that synthesize data from multiple polls over time, including one from the Pew Research Center called "Trends in Political Values and Core Attitudes: 1987–2007."[22] In another 2007 report, the nonprofit organization Campaign for America's Future compiled more recent polls administered by survey research organizations such as Gallup and Pew, as well as news organizations such as the *Wall Street Journal* and the *Los Angeles Times,* to examine comprehensively Americans' views on a wide range of economic, social, and military issues.[23] The polls synthesized in these reports—and in hundreds of other individual polling studies—overwhelmingly contradict widespread assumptions about a conservative, masculinized American majority. We report on these polls in such detail because the results are counterintuitive for many people, who see a conservative country. A close look at the polls reveals that, while the government pursues masculinized policies, ordinary Americans want a feminized progressivism.

Data on support for government social programs are a good beginning point, because they are a sensitive indicator of the feminized values of empathy, equality, and community. The Pew 2007 study of core values shows that 69 percent of voters agree that "government should care for those who cannot care for themselves." Likewise 54 percent agree that "government should help the needy even if it means greater debt."[24] In a period of high personal and public deficits, this shows a feminized majority committed to a generous safety net, but polls show a broader feminized commitment to help all citizens. For example, while men are more likely than women to prefer a smaller government with fewer services, 58 percent of Americans, reflecting millions of men as well as a majority of women, think the government should overall be doing more for citizens, not less.[25] A 2004 National Elections Studies poll showed that twice as many Americans support more government services and more spending compared to those who support fewer services and less spending, even if it means an increase in taxes. The same poll showed that the percentage of Americans who support the feminized position of more services and spending increased from 23 percent in 1982 to 43 percent in 2004, not yet quite a majority, while the percent opposing it dropped from 32 percent in 1982 to 20 percent in 2004.[26]

The issue of health care provides a striking example of the feminized majority's commitment to provide help for all citizens. While politicians worry that promoting a system of nationalized health care is career suicide, multiple polls show that a majority of Americans want the government to guarantee health care for all citizens—and are willing to make sacrifices to see it happen. A *New York Times/CBS News* poll taken in March 2007 found that 60 percent of Americans would pay higher taxes to ensure that all citizens had coverage.[27] A CNN/Opinion Research Corporation poll from May 2007 asking the same question found an even higher majority—64 percent.[28] A Gallup poll from late 2006 showed that 69 percent of Americans feel it is the "responsibility" of the federal government to provide health care coverage to all its citizens.[29] This data suggests that a majority of Americans have adopted the feminized ideals of community and empathy and believe that the government has a responsibility to help their fellow citizens preserve their health.

A majority of Americans believe that government should do more to protect workers' wages. Increasing the minimum wage is supported by a huge majority of Americans. A December 2006 AP/AOL News poll showed that 80 percent of Americans support a government-mandated increase in the minimum wage, with only 18 percent opposed.[30] A *Los Angeles Times*/Bloomberg poll, also from late 2006, found 77 percent of Americans want Congress to pass legislation to raise the minimum wage.[31] A CNN poll in August 2006 found 86 percent in support and only 13 percent in opposition.[32] These statistics reflect the feminized values of community and empathy: People should lift up their friends and neighbors and give a hand to those in need.

Americans are also uneasy about corporate power and the increasing divide between rich and poor, as reflected in their views about taxes. A Gallup poll from April 2007 showed that 71 percent of Americans feel that taxes on corporations are too low, and 66 percent feel that taxes on upper-income people are too low.[33] A 2005 *NBC News* poll showed that 54 percent believe that corporations pay "lower than their fair share of taxes" while only 4 percent believe they pay "more."[34] An *NBC News/Wall Street Journal* poll from 2005 found that a majority of Americans feel that Bush's tax cuts, largely serving the rich, were "not worth it."[35] Americans are turning away from the masculinized perspective that individualism is virtuous and that the rich deserve their wealth.

Americans also support unions. A 2007 Pew poll showed that 56 percent are favorable to unions, while only 33 percent are unfavorable.[36] A 2006 Gallup poll finds similar results: 59 percent favorable to unions compared to 29 percent unfavorable.[37] In the same poll, 52 percent of people say they generally side with unions in labor disputes compared to 34 percent who take the side of the company.[38] Unions embody the feminized values of cooperation, equality, and *Together We Can.*

Perhaps American workers know they are living in frightening times. The 1980s and 1990s represented an era of corporations consolidating power: Multiple corporate mergers resulted in monopolies or oligarchies; free trade legislation led to endemic outsourcing and layoffs;

and stagnant wages caused more Americans to sink into poverty as CEOs reaped unprecedented bonus-laden salaries—sometimes reaching hundreds of millions of dollars even as their companies sank, as in the cases of Enron and Tyco. In the face of such greed and corruption, the feminized values of equality, community, and cooperation resonate more than ever to men as well as women.

Americans also share an increasingly feminized outlook on social issues. Comparing current polls to those from decades past shows how the country is changing on charged social issues such as gay and lesbian rights, women's rights, and affirmative action. In 1987, for example, 51 percent of Americans felt that school boards "ought to have the right to fire teachers who are known homosexuals," and a 1977 Gallup poll showed that only 56 percent believed that homosexuals should have equal job rights.[39] In contrast, a 2006 Gallup poll finds a robust 89 percent of Americans believe that homosexuals should have equal job rights.[40] As noted earlier, more women than men support overturning "Don't Ask, Don't Tell" military policy, but a Pew poll shows that 60 percent of *all* Americans support gay and lesbian soldiers openly serving in the military.[41]

Support of equality for gays and lesbians, women, and racial minorities is a core marker of the feminized sensibility. On the highly charged issue of same-sex marriage, a feminized majority does not yet support same-sex marriage itself. Gallup polling in 2007 shows 46 percent in favor and 53 percent opposed.[42] Other polls, including a 2007 Pew poll, show a smaller percentage, 37 percent, supporting same-sex marriage with 55 percent opposed.[43] But if we look at the percentage supporting either same-sex marriage or civil unions codifying legal rights for gay and lesbian couples, a 2007 CNN poll shows that 50 percent support either same-sex marriage or civil unions.[44] A generation ago, hardly any Americans supported same-sex marriage, because being homosexual was seen as shameful and therefore mostly hidden. For example, a 1982 Gallup poll showed that only 32 percent of Americans viewed "homosexuality as an acceptable lifestyle."[45] Today, the feminized majority increasingly embraces gay and lesbian Americans and gay rights as an expression of its core value of equality.

A majority of feminized Americans now embrace women's rights. In 1987, only 28 percent of Americans "completely disagreed" that "women should return to their traditional roles in society."[46] By 2007, 51 percent "completely disagreed" and 75 percent disagreed, either completely or mostly.[47] Likewise, in 1972, a National Election Studies poll showed that only 47 percent of Americans believed that "women should have an equal role with men in running business, industry and government."[48] By 2004, that number soared to 78 percent.[49] A solid majority of women and a majority of men now support women's new roles and rights.

The most charged issue about women's rights is abortion. Despite continuing controversy, and the intense views of those who equate abortion with murder, a majority of Americans—57 percent, according to a 2007 *ABC News/Washington Post* poll—want to keep abortion legal "in all or most cases."[50] An August 2007 Quinnipiac poll found 62 percent of Americans agreeing and 32 percent disagreeing with the *Roe v. Wade* decision that "establishes a woman's right" to abortion.[51] A May 2007 Gallup poll showed that only 35 percent of Americans support overturning a woman's constitutional right to abortion.[52] The feminized majority specifically affirms abortion as a "right" that protects not just the woman but constitutional ideals of privacy and social well-being. But the majority is sensitive to concerns about the adverse social impact of abortion on demand. A 2007 *CBS News/New York Times* poll showed that a plurality of 41 percent seek "stricter limits" on the availability of abortion even though 75 percent, a clear majority, want to retain the right to abortion guaranteed by *Roe v. Wade*.[53]

A growing feminized majority also supports civil rights for racial and ethnic minorities. In 1987, when Pew polls asked whether "it's all right for blacks and whites to date each other," 48 percent agreed; by 2007, 83 percent agreed, with the trend unwaveringly upward and a visceral indicator of a new tolerance and feminized social egalitarianism.[54] Affirmative action, another key expression of a feminized commitment to support and nurture the underdog, is also widely supported as in the interest of the whole society. A 2003 Pew poll regarding affirmative action—taken in the midst of a Supreme Court battle over the subject—showed that 57 percent of Americans support programs "which give special preferences to qualified blacks, women and other minorities in hiring and education."[55]

A Zogby poll taken right after the 2004 elections asked Americans what is the most "urgent moral question" in the nation.[56] While abortion and same-sex marriage had gathered all the headlines, and reflected the conservative religious moral agenda, only 16 percent of voters answered "abortion" and 12 percent "same-sex marriage." The majority said the "most urgent moral question" was either "greed and materialism" (33 percent) or "poverty and economic justice" (31 percent). Together, 64 percent of Americans expressed the feminized majority's real moral concerns: a focus on injustice and inequality that harms the entire society.

The most dramatic examples of feminized values becoming majoritarian emerge with issues of militarism and foreign policy. As we've noted, women are more likely to support diplomacy over force as a way to solve problems. However, a 2005 poll showed that 64 percent of Americans—again, reflecting millions of men as well as women—feel the United States "should emphasize diplomatic and economic efforts over military efforts in fighting the War on Terror."[57] In 2007, the percentage rose to 67 percent.[58] More broadly, a 2005 Pew poll showed that 55 percent of Americans agree that "the best way to ensure peace is through diplomacy," while only 30 percent said the best way to secure peace is "military strength."[59] Poll numbers over time suggest that Americans are increasingly adopting the feminized position that violence is not a viable way to secure peace.[60]

It makes sense for the feminized values of diplomacy and international cooperation to become the norm. Thousands and thousands of Americans have lost family members in the wars in Iraq and Afghanistan, yet the regions are no closer to being stabilized. Reports from Iraq suggest that the war has actually created *more* terrorists. And in the midst of this desperate situation, some fear that the Bush administration is setting up Iran as America's next military target. After the carnage in Iraq, it is not surprising that Americans are leery of using firepower to tamp down Iran's alleged terrorist support network. The masculinized view that aggression secures victory doesn't seem to fit reality.

A February 2007 Gallup poll showed that the majority of Americans not only prefer diplomacy to violence *but also are beginning to challenge American hegemony itself.* This challenge is not firmly established—the same poll finds 60 percent of Americans saying that the United States should continue to be the country with the most powerful military. But when Gallup asked a differently worded question, about what role America should play in the world, only 15 percent said "the leading role." A remarkable 58 percent majority said "a major role but not the leading role."[61] This is an explicit rejection of American hegemony and of elite concepts of American empire.

As the situation in Iraq becomes more desperate, Americans increasingly want our soldiers out. A *CBS News* poll from 9 September 2007 showed 62 percent of Americans feel the U.S. invasion of Iraq was a "mistake."[62] A full 53

percent say that Iraq will "never" become a stable democracy. And poll after poll—including those from the
Washington Post/ABC News, USA Today/Gallup, and *CBS
News/New York Times*—show that a majority of Americans want a firm deadline for withdrawing American
forces from the region.[63]

Polls also show that it will take a lot more than ma-
nipulated reports about yellowcake from Niger—one of the
ways the Bush administration misled Congress to authorize the Iraq War—to gain public approval for the next
war; despite a calculated fear campaign from the Bush
administration, in April 2006, CNN/Opinion Research
Corporation found that a full 63 percent of Americans
oppose war with Iran.[64] This is not to say that Americans
support Iran creating a nuclear weapons program. Polls
show that Americans, in fact, desire an end to *all* nuclear
weapons programs—including that of the United States.
A Pew report released in November 2005 shows that 70
percent of Americans support a "multilateral disarma-
ment treaty."[65] Americans want changes in international
relations that will usher in a new era of nonviolence. The
nuclear arms race of the cold war was a masculinized
competition to see which boys had the most toys, and
most Americans don't want to play that game again.
An increasing number of women and men are adopting
feminized ideals and goals, and are demanding a peaceful future for their children.

We argue that these changes in values show a new
American majority that rejects the masculinized values
from American history and supports new feminized values. This shift of major dimensions represents a threat to
the historic masculinized systems of American capitalism
and empire, secured by rampant individualism, and to the
traditional American Dream. Our nation, constructed as
an individualistic capitalist hierarchy, rewards (in theory)
those who work the hardest with the biggest rewards.

By pursuing feminized ideals, such as egalitarianism and nonviolence, Americans are softening the founding principles of our country.

When a country becomes inhospitable to its citizens and unwilling to help its people in need, and when an aggressive foreign policy fails and threatens citizens rather than protects them, many citizens will reexamine the values and dreams handed down to them. Feminized values lead to economic policy that gives underprivileged and middle-class Americans a chance to succeed. The *Together We Can* philosophy becomes more appealing to both women and men. Feminized values create foreign policy that values human rights and makes America a partner in the global community, again enhancing the appeal of *Together We Can* for all Americans.

Americans still pursue self-interest and profit. But as the feminized majority grows, more ordinary citizens—both women and men—believe this pursuit needs to be carried out under different rules. A feminized vision requires a fairer, more egalitarian, and less violent social order. The new feminized majority sees the need for changes in the underlying social and moral fabric, helping explain why a huge majority of Americans today say America is moving in the wrong direction under President Bush and the Republicans. As America's economic and military crises lead more men to join women in embracing feminized values, a rising feminized majority can transform not only the Democratic Party but also America itself.

CHAPTER FIVE

Sex, Class, and Values

In the wake of the 2004 election, many authors and bloggers implored the Democratic Party to adopt a values-based platform and reframe issues such as health care, poverty, and education under a "progressive moral values" heading. We agree with these writers on the need to reinterpret values outside of a conservative religious framework. However, they miss a crucial aspect of the evangelical values strategy: a moral compass. Republicans frequently claim that their policies reflect biblical values, and Republican candidates can use Christian rhetoric—either through explicit quotations or implicit buzzwords—in speeches pushing these policies. Whether Republicans use the Bible or manipulate the Bible is a different question, and of particular concern to the religious left. Whatever their intentions, by crafting policy that supposedly follows biblical law, Republicans appear transparent and consistent. They seem guided by principles larger than themselves.

Progressive values strategists lack similar text on which to build. Although the term *progressive values* seems clear enough to people on the left, what exactly does it mean? Every progressive would give a different answer when asked to define progressive values. This ambiguity makes it very difficult to create policy. Voters find it difficult to latch onto a party that lacks a clear program.

Feminized values provide the moral foundation that progressives need. We have already shown that feminized values will lead to a different kind of America, with a strong social welfare system and a foreign policy doctrine based on peace and diplomacy. In this sense, a feminized values platform will lead to the same ends as the various "progressive values" platforms proposed by other writers. However, a feminized values platform also provides the necessary compass for the formation of a new Democratic Party. To create a cohesive message, Democrats must understand the gendered values and feminized mindset that are the strongest moral basis of their progressive positions. In this chapter, we explore the historical reasons why women embrace feminized values, why feminized values transform into progressive policy, the relationship between gender and class values, and why feminized values have become the most important generator of values-based progressive politics.

By organizing values in terms of gender, we are not trying to prove that women are the carriers of these values and men are not—or that gender is the only crucible of values for progressives. Race and class are also key incubators of values and a critical part of our story. We want to show that, historically, women have been socialized to support the values that create "progressive" policy, while men have been taught to reject these values. By understanding where these values come from, we can gain a better understanding of feminized thought and learn how to apply these values to a Democratic policy agenda that promotes what we call "feminized populism." We can then discern which women and men will lead the feminized majority movement.

The Origins of Feminized Values

Gender gap research suggests that one gender consistently supports progressive morality and policy. Women and men are socialized into values based on their gender,

and gender gap data reflect how these values are manifested in the political realm. Feminized values, in the context of politics, lead to support for progressive policies. We
should not forget, however, that feminized values affect all
aspects of women's lives, political and nonpolitical. Women
take these values into account when making decisions
about work, family, and relationships. They also carry
them into the voting booth and use them to form opinions
about what kind of America they want to live in.

Feminized values represent a combination of women's
subordination and women's liberation. Some feminized
values stretch back centuries before capitalism, when
men forced women to take care of the hearth and home.
Although we have moved well beyond traditional patriarchy, we still socialize women into roles and values involving caretaking and family and men into roles and values
involving domination and violence. This patriarchal moral
bedrock continues to influence our values.

Other feminized values were a response to women's
subjugation under the capitalist system. Compared to
patriarchy, capitalism is a new system superimposing
itself in the last few centuries on the ancient patriarchal order. Capitalism brings a new master morality of
self-interest, reinforcing men's traditional values of aggression and moving them from tribalism toward their
current narrative of *Alone I Will.* But because capitalism
continued to assign the main family and caretaking
responsibilities to women, it perpetuated a gendered
value system reflecting patriarchal morals. As capitalism
evolved, and feminism opened up new opportunities for
women, gendered divisions of labor were softened, but
women continued to be held responsible for caretaking
and family. Women entered the labor force, but with different overall roles in society. The feminized narrative of
Together We Can shows that women are not as tightly
intertwined as men with the capitalist morality of "me,
me, me." This is hardly surprising, because, despite great

strides, women remain a subordinated majority tied to caretaking roles.

In this chapter, we look more closely at how and why women continue to hold feminized values—ones that clash with capitalist morality—in our thoroughly capitalized society. But we need to note at the outset something unique about women's values, something that separates them morally from the naked self-interest of our economic system. Put simply, women's values—because they are rooted in ideals of community, empathy, and concern for others—are about more than women. They lead beyond the narrow interest of women to the care and tending of society at large.

Why Women's Values Are Not Capitalist Values

Women's values lead to progressive politics because women are integrated into our social and economic order differently than men. They live in capitalism but are not entirely of it. Women's values generate a moral foundation for progressive opposition because: (1) women are subordinated in the existing order, and (2) their movement against their unequal position expresses values that can benefit all disadvantaged groups and promote equality and peace.

The gender gap data prompt a much broader discussion about the social forces that dominate capitalist society and the roles that traditionally oppressed peoples—such as women, minorities, and the poor—play in capitalist society. All oppressed groups have a role to play in transforming America, although in some other societies women's values do not play the same leading role. In Europe, for example, the working class has provided the moral foundation for progressive politics. But for reasons discussed shortly, women and feminized values have emerged as a basis for *American* progressive politics that can challenge capitalist as well as patriarchal priorities.

Researchers agree that the gender gap is the result of women asserting political independence and asserting values that transcend capitalist morality. Women respond to inequality with an assertion of their own feminized moral perspective. So both the persistent inequality of women in the economic system and the disjunction between women's roles and capitalist roles explain why women's values are transforming America.

Many Americans might question our claim that our economic system subjugates women or has hindered their liberation. Capitalism, on its face, rewards people strictly for their merit; it claims to be fair and meritocratic. Although once confined to the home, women have now achieved positions in the highest levels of politics and business. Our secretary of state is a woman of color, and women now make up over half of many law school and medical school classes.

Although women's lot is improving, their wages are still lower than men's, and women remain the largest group of poor people in the nation. Gender inequality is far from disappearing, both in terms of women's economic roles and the incomes they earn. As income differentials intensify, with the richest 1 percent of Americans controlling 42 percent of national wealth, class interests are increasingly important in American politics—and the Democrats can win and transform the economic order only with a strong populist agenda. Paradoxically, though, it is women's values rather than class values that will create a progressive politics capable of doing just that.

Women's values strongly dispose them toward progressive economic policies, even if they are affluent. Women in all socioeconomic classes are more progressive than their male counterparts, even the wealthiest and most highly educated women who benefit personally from economic inequality. Women of all classes, that is, carry values that lead toward progressive attitudes, while men in all classes are socialized to values more consistent with the capitalist order.

Because many leftist discussions of class are gender blind, they are incomplete and unrepresentative of both the female and male experience. A woman does not experience wealth in the same way as a man. Feminist Kate Millett wrote several decades ago that "whatever the class of her birth and education, the female has fewer permanent class associations than does the male. Economic dependency renders her affiliations with any class a tangential, vicarious, and temporary matter."[1] While women certainly have become more economically independent since Millett wrote this essay, income and wealth disparities continue to exist between men and women, and women are differently and less securely perched on the class ladder than men. In any event, their gendered values and social roles lead them to see the overall system in a way different than men do, wherever they may be perched.

The values into which women and men are socialized in a capitalist system help explain which gender is more likely to succeed—and how they will respond to success or failure. Feminist theorist Heidi Hartmann writes, "If we examine the characteristics of men ... competitive, rationalistic, dominating—they are much like our description of the dominant values of capitalist society."[2] Men, whether rich or poor, are socialized into masculinized values, which are closely intertwined with capitalist values. In turn, men of all socioeconomic levels exhibit capitalistic traits that privilege them in American society. Male aggression—highly valued in capitalism—is manifested in boardrooms, factories, and bedrooms. Domestic violence statistics show the dark side of men's socialized values and implicate men of all classes.

While our economic system increasingly oppresses men and women in lower socioeconomic classes, only boys are socialized to develop attitudes that capitalist society highly values. Girls, on the other hand, are socialized to be nurturing, compassionate, and empathetic—traits that are less desirable in corporate America. Feminized values, therefore, are shaped by class position but originate in gendered roles and inequalities. Certainly, we cannot extract a woman's gender identity from her racial and socioeconomic identities, because each of these factors creates a person's overall sense of self. Yet, there is no denying that women are socialized into a gender-specific set of values, and these values cause women to have a different relationship with capitalism than men.

The feminized value system can be understood on two levels. First, it is a reaction to the structural disadvantages faced by women in a patriarchal capitalist system. Social class theorists and feminists agree that women are subordinated because their labor is devalued. While feminists argue that this precedes capitalism, they nonetheless understand how poor women and poor men share economic oppression in today's economic order. The second way of understanding the feminized majority is by examining the attitudes that create capitalist culture. It is no coincidence that the highly prized capitalist values of competitiveness, rationality, and toughness are the same attitudes into which boys are socialized. Capitalist culture and masculine culture are closely intertwined, and women's values conflict with both.

Because the feminized majority's mind-set is a gendered concept, women are fittingly in the best position to launch a progressive movement against the system that doesn't appreciate or reward their values. However, because a woman is not born into her gender, but is socialized into it, a man is equally capable of becoming part of the feminized majority movement by rejecting certain masculinized values. The feminized viewpoint depends not on a person's biology, but on the attitudes he or she carries into the polling booth.

Feminized Values and Class Politics

We have shown that policies based on feminized values will lead to a more inclusive America, an America less divided by class and an America more welcoming to those on the lower end of the socioeconomic ladder. Because a majority of Americans support moving the nation in this direction, perhaps these trends point to a values revolution based on *class*, not gender. In light of recent outsourcing, corporate mergers, and the Enron debacle, perhaps America is undergoing a class-based solidarity movement against the country's economic elite. Maybe average American workers are finally coming together to say, "This system is failing us."

The values of equality and solidarity, after all, are not the sole province of feminized culture. Historically, these values are associated with the working class. Since the time of Karl Marx, people on the left have understood that the working class has the potential to come together and fight for their ideals in the face of greed and corruption. The key is motivating workers to think as a group, develop values together, and create a social movement.

In Europe, where working-class culture is nurtured and highly developed, the working class is an important bearer of values. The Labour Party of the United Kingdom, for example, historically runs candidates on working-class values. The party's constitution notes: "The Labour Party is a democratic socialist party. It believes that by the strength of our common endeavour we achieve more than we achieve alone, so as to create for each of us the means to realise our true potential and for all of us a community in which power, wealth and opportunity are in the hands of the many, not the few."[3]

In Sweden, Denmark, France, and other social democratic nations on the Continent, labor parties are even stronger than in England. The United States has no equivalent to European labor parties. The Democratic

Party, while certainly more friendly to workers than the Republican Party, is not a workers' party. No mainstream political party exists on a foundation of working-class values like those exhibited in the Labour Party constitution.

Working-class culture is also strong in Europe because of the enduring strength of unions and the historic prevalence of places, such as union halls and pubs, where workers congregate after work.[4] These places create public spaces for workers to meet, socialize, and build a common mind-set. Over many years, these settings nourished a working-class moral compass that helped shape progressive movements in European politics. *Class can become a potent source of values and values-driven politics, and in Europe it has done just that.*

Capitalism and the promise of the American Dream makes it difficult for working-class values to develop, because Americans are acculturated into the idea that America is a classless society. The American master narrative is that those at the top of the socioeconomic ladder have earned their place. If someone is in financial dire straits, he or she must work harder. No one in the working class should view his or her position as permanent. Upward mobility is inevitable in America, so long as a person is willing to put in the effort to succeed. These capitalistic attitudes, which were nurtured early on by the endless frontier and the mythical ability of every American to get land or start a business, make it difficult for the working class to develop and maintain cultural values of its own.

Of course, the working class does assert itself in American politics—and the Democratic Party sometimes embraces class values. Unions, for example, are still extremely important in election cycles and as part of the Democratic Party. Unions give voice to the needs and concerns of the working class and provide a countervailing force against business advocacy groups.[5] They are outspoken on issues concerning the minimum wage, free trade agreements, and workers' rights. They play such a crucial role in the political process that it's scary to imagine an America without them. Nevertheless, unions do not serve the same purpose in American elections as the feminized majority. Unions operate as an interest group, whereas the feminized majority is a values-generating body of Americans. Unions seek higher wages and benefits for their members but have not historically promoted a broad agenda of equality and peace. American unions, especially in the crafts and trades, have often protected turf and privileges for their members by excluding and exploiting others, especially racial minorities and women.[6]

A working-class culture exists in the United States, but it is fragmented and relatively weak compared to its counterpart in most European nations. In Europe, class generates a powerful value system supporting broad social reform, but in the United States it creates an interest-driven politics for narrower social ends. In America, class interests are becoming increasingly vital as a globalized capitalism makes life harsher for workers. Class interests are also increasingly important in shaping voters' behavior and may override the impact of values. Many lower-class men with masculinized values, as we show later, vote Democratic purely because they have narrow interests in a higher minimum wage, not because they have feminized values. Similarly, many religiously conservative poor or working women vote Democratic for the same reason: their economic self-interest. Interests as well as values shape political behavior—and both are legitimate and compelling.

But to achieve a progressive politics, we need an underlying values-driven vision that coalesces class interests into a coherent universalistic moral philosophy that can guide the Democratic Party and a larger social movement, bringing together many different groups for change. Class values and working-class cultures exist in the United States but they are not strong enough to generate this vision on their own, despite the growing class polarization and increased importance of class interests. This reality reflects the overwhelming strength of American capitalist culture; the political hegemony of business in politics, media, and society; the division of the working class by race and gender; and the corresponding weakness of working-class institutions and worldviews.

As a result, the United States has been described as "exceptionalist," that is, different in its politics than other developed nations. Its lack of a strong working-class culture and politics explains why socialist movements were so weak in America even as they became so strong throughout Europe. *But workers in America need the same social justice and progressive politics that class movements—based on strong class-based moral values—have produced in Europe. In the United States, the values that will guide this new politics are rooted in the rising feminized majority and a program of feminized populism.*

Feminized values can play this role for several reasons. In the United States, while workers are confused about class identity, women have a strong identity as women. They share a history of oppression rooted in their gender, their family roles, and their economic position as workers. Moreover, they are now the majority of the working class and the poor. More broadly, women are the majority of the population at large, and thus feminized values always have huge potential clout in politics.

Another key reason involves the critical role of the family in politics. Both political parties claim to protect American families, especially children. But a new crisis of the family is exposing the weakness of Republicans' morals and the strength of feminized values. While union membership erodes and companies move jobs overseas, the family is under great strain; women and men are both struggling with tricky balancing acts involving time, money, children, and love. This crisis puts a disproportionate burden on women and is becoming more relevant than ever to political discourse. Because women's attitudes are tied closely to nurturance and family care, feminized values are important today; they are a natural counterweight to the conservative vision of "family values" that Republicans claim grows out of the Bible.

Unlike the concerns of interest groups, feminized values pertain to all issues—domestic and international. Feminized values extend well beyond stereotypical "women's issues" like child care, health care, and education, and include war, globalization, and workers' rights. Although feminized values often serve the interests of the working class, they extend to a concern with peace, the environment, and the well-being of all peoples. Feminized values are universalizing values in progressive politics.

The Feminized Path
to Race and Class Values

Although the feminized majority is a gender-based movement, gender exists only as part of a person's complete biography. Gender intersects with a person's other defining characteristics, such as race, age, religion, education, and class. The melding of these different aspects creates identity. While all women historically have been oppressed, women of color have faced unique challenges. Capitalism, after all, was created in a racist as well as patriarchal framework. The most egregious error of the modern feminist movement has been the dismissal of these women's concerns as "divisive." In her essay "The Master's Tools Will Never Dismantle the Master's House," Audre Lorde writes, "Advocating the mere tolerance of difference between women is the grossest reformism. It is a total denial of the creative function of difference in our lives. Difference must not be merely tolerated, but seen as a fund of necessary polarities between which our creativity can spark like a dialectic."[7] While women share many commonalities because of their oppression in a patriarchal system, some women are far more privileged than others due to their race or class.

Even after controlling for race, studies show a gender gap exists for most political issues. However, one could instead control for gender to prove that a race gap exists for many political issues as well. In fact, the much-hyped gender gap in the 2004 presidential election would have disappeared if not for the support of women of color; 55 percent of white women voted for Bush.[8] As 53 percent of the electorate, women exercise a particularly important influence over elections and their core values are majoritarian. They cannot create progressive change without more attention to race values carried by African Americans and other racial or ethnic minorities.

The core value of equality arises out of inequalities suffered most deeply by racial minorities in America. Women have experienced profound inequality, but white women did not experience Southern slavery and other horrific forms of inequality that African Americans did. Women's experiences, though, can help sensitize them to these indignities and help sensitize all Americans to the values that are rooted in race as well as class.

The relation of feminized values to values generated by race and class experience is exceptionally important. The feminized majority is disproportionately composed of racial minorities and the working classes. Racial minorities and working-class groups within the feminized majority must assert their own values—bred out of their gender, race, and class experiences—in order to help guide the feminized majority itself. Whites and upper-middle-class members of the feminized majority must open themselves to these other sources of values. Working-class women and women of color can help teach white and upper-middle-class women in the feminized majority that their own gender-based experiences are only one prism through which liberating values can be expressed. Feminized values and the *Together We Can* philosophy requires embracing values of those who have suffered racial and class discrimination; these are inseparable from the experience of the feminized majority itself and essential to the emancipatory potential of feminized politics.

Feminized values must be a path in America to rediscovering and addressing the moral crises bred by race and class injustice. Feminized values of community and equality require the most urgent attention to American racial and class crises. If the Democratic Party does not address these crises, it does not understand feminized values or the feminized majority. And the feminized majority itself must urgently listen to its own working-class members and members of color to awaken itself to the full meaning of its own morality.

A feminized Democratic Party will become more like the European social democratic parties that draw explicitly on class values and class politics, while also integrating race values that have been largely ignored in Europe. A truly feminized Democratic agenda will help transform the Democratic Party from a second business party to a labor party. And it will become more—not less—a party of African Americans, Latinos, and other minorities. Feminized values and a feminized majority strategy reshuffle the Democratic deck to become the party of all those who have endured inequalities and sufferings. Women are the largest such group, but have no privileged moral claim over other historically disadvantaged groups even within the context of feminized values.

Feminized or Feminist?

"Feminized" values—those into which women are typically socialized—must be differentiated from feminism, broadly defined as an ideology promoting equality between the sexes but with multiple nuanced visions. Briefly examining some of the different categories of feminism allows us better to understand the intersection of feminized and feminist politics.

Most people associate feminism with fights for political and legal reforms—from the suffrage movements of the early twentieth century to *Roe v. Wade* and the Equal Rights Amendment in the 1970s. These events provide examples of using mainstream (or "liberal") feminism as a tool for directly improving the lives of women in tangible ways. This kind of feminism is different from feminized politics just as class-based politics differs from feminized politics: It is a movement based on self-interest, not on overarching values that transcend the injustices facing a particular group.

Feminist movements do not always promote what we call feminized values, which are universalistic and require attention to values linked to racial and class injustice. American feminist movements have sometimes promoted white women's interests and ignored the needs of women of color, and at other times advanced interests of affluent women and ignored the needs of poor and working-class women. Such feminist movements promoting only narrow women's interests do not carry the feminized values that are the basis of the rising feminized majority.

Some kinds of feminism closely align with feminized politics. Radical feminism, one strand of second-wave feminism that developed in the 1960s and 1970s, for example, calls for a critical examination of the complex ways that male hegemony is established and maintained. Radical feminist theories advocated more than bureaucratic reforms to fight patriarchy; some called for dismantling the institution of marriage and the nuclear family, others supported overthrowing capitalism. Third-wave feminism, which developed in the 1980s and 1990s and is now popular among many young feminists, also brings a wide-angle vision to feminist politics. Following in the spirit of thinkers like Patricia Hill Collins, Audre Lorde, and bell hooks—and shaped by poststructuralist thinking about the importance of race and class, difference and subjectivity—third-wave feminism argues that the oppression of women is intertwined with the problems of women of color and of the working class.[9] It also argues that feminist thinking offers a liberating way of thinking about all cultural, social, and political issues, not just those related to gender.

Kalpana Krishnamurthy, age twenty-five, is codirector of the New York–based Third Wave Foundation that works with young women mainly in their twenties. She sees feminism evolving in a way that feminist journalist Jennifer Friedlin captures evocatively: "from a movement focused on a handful of issues into a movement that pervades all aspects of society." Continues Friedlin, "While feminists in the second wave were more focused on fighting for gender equality in the workplace, abortion rights and economic parity, today's activists say they are looking at a wider range of topics through the feminist lens."[10]

Friedlin sees third-wave feminists, such as Krishnamurthy, as "having the freedom to offer their unique perspectives on everything from arts and culture to prison reform."[11] Krishnamurthy replies: "I think that the impact of the feminist movement was in helping women to achieve a voice ... Now, we are articulating that voice in a multiplicity of ways."[12]

While not all third-wavers are political activists, their pluralistic, wide-angle contemporary feminist approach aligns with feminized politics because it (1) emphasizes the social construction and differences among feminisms, (2) illustrates that different forms of oppression are related and come from deep-seated societal conditions and beliefs that are not easy to change, and (3) concludes that feminist politics is not only about gender. Like third-wave feminism, a feminized political ideology pushes for more than legislative reform about women's rights; it demands a revolution of American values and a drastic reevaluation of the nation's political, economic, and military institutions. It implies a social movement that unites women—and many men—across gender, class, and race lines for broad social change. It also implies a highly pluralistic movement that respects difference and does not promote a single "feminist line."

Feminized politics as well as much of third-wave feminism transcend the typical identity politics associated with women and the gender gap. The new feminized majority is concerned with broad social reforms, reforms that will undoubtedly benefit women as part of a much larger transformative movement. As we noted earlier, interest groups are extraordinarily important in politics; without advocacy groups fighting for the rights of women, the United States would be much worse off. Yet, feminized politics is a different kind of politics, based on values, and may lead to broad social reforms for the benefit of average citizens—women and men alike. It provides a moral foundation for movements to champion women's needs—as well as class and race justice—as part of a fight to save, nurture, and liberate society itself.

Gender, Class, and the Feminized Majority

Gender is the primary source of values motivating the feminized majority, but class remains especially important for understanding why voters are part of the growing movement. By arranging voters by gender and class, we create intersections that help us understand why different feminized majority voters carry feminized attitudes. The intersections look like a two-by-two matrix, made up of upper-class men, upper-class women, lower-class men, and lower-class women (see Figure 5.1). These different

Upper-class men	Upper-class women
Lower-class men	Lower-class women

Figure 5.1

identities are affected by capitalist masculinized attitudes in different ways. For example, upper-class men are economically privileged by the institutions of capitalism and sociologically privileged by capitalist masculinized values. Upper-class women, who are structurally (or economically) privileged in capitalism, are still disadvantaged by their socialization into feminized values. Lower-class men are privileged by masculine capitalist values, but disadvantaged by structural capitalism. Finally, lower-class women are disadvantaged both structurally and attitudinally.

Although the American electorate is much too complex to compartmentalize into four categories, the matrix is useful for understanding where the feminized majority gets the most support. If lower-class men experience structural or economic oppression, and upper-class women experience oppression because of their values, then we can see how each subset of the electorate is affected by capitalism. Naturally, lower-class women are at the intersection of both kinds of oppression.

It should also be noted that the table is not made of four equal parts, because the four subsets of the electorate do not contribute equally to the feminized majority. Upper-class men, for example, benefit the most from capitalist values. They also have the most to lose if capitalism is restrained in favor of a feminized values strategy. Therefore, upper-class men are the most likely to be underrepresented in the feminized majority. Conversely, lower-class women have the most to gain from a feminized values strategy. These women are disadvantaged in terms of their material wealth, as well as in the disjuncture between their gendered values and the capitalist values that are rewarded in America. The feminized majority can therefore expect vast support from women in this category.

A large portion of the feminized majority support comes from lower-class men. A man can adopt a feminized worldview because, as mentioned before, a person's gender is constructed using many elements besides his or her value system, and a person's value system comprises many things other than his or her gender. Working-class and union men, for example, who support raising wage levels because of their concern for the well-being of the poor and working class, have an egalitarian and community-oriented worldview that grows out of—or converges with—the feminized *Together We Can* morality. Their fears about free market economic competition and individualism reflect the same fears that women have about unrestrained capitalism. In Europe, where working-class culture is strong, millions of such working-class men are socialized into equality and community values mainly by unions themselves—an experience that some American male workers share. But in America, the overwhelming majority of working men are not in unions and think of themselves as middle class rather than working class. Those who believe in equality or community, then, are less likely to be shaped by a working-class morality, as in Europe, but by a feminized culture transmitted by their mothers, female teachers, or fellow women workers.[13]

Despite their weakness and historically narrow interest concerns, American unions offer a countervailing force against free market capitalism and are one of the few American sources of class values.[14] They were founded on class principles that overlap extensively with feminized morality. For example, the preamble to the AFL-CIO constitution reads, "We resolve to fulfill the yearning of the human spirit for liberty, justice and community. ... We dedicate ourselves to improving the lives of working families, bringing fairness and dignity to the workplace and securing social equity in the Nation."[15] If the feminized majority created a constitution, the preamble would include many of the same values. As women have become a majority in some unions, their values increasingly broaden today's American labor union morality to include a feminized vision of equality and peace for all.

Values Voters, Self-Interest, and a Feminized Democratic Strategy

People who join unions have varied levels of support for union principles. Some steadfastly believe in the community of the working class and will make sacrifices to promote solidarity with union brothers and sisters. These are *values voters*—driven by moral concerns. Others join out of pragmatism, viewing a union as the best way to achieve their personal goals of a better job, higher wages, and better working conditions. These are *interest voters*—driven by self-interest. Just as people join unions for different reasons, voters align themselves with the feminized majority for reasons that may involve either values or self-interest. The feminized majority consists only of those sharing its feminized values and voting them. But one of its strengths when seen as a guide for

Democratic strategy is that it also brings into the Democratic fold many "interest voters" along with feminized values voters.

Many working-class men have masculinized values and don't fit the feminized majority moral framework, yet will still vote in line with it. Imagine a working-class man who supports raising the minimum wage for *non-feminized* majority reasons. His worldview is not based on the values of community and empathy; his ideal country is one where he is richer and can buy more things. He feels his wife should be home with their children, and by making more money, he can make that happen. He is socially conservative on all issues related to equality. But, as someone structurally oppressed or economically disadvantaged by capitalism, he votes for Democratic candidates and helps the feminized majority.

This man clearly does not hold a feminized worldview. He votes individualistically, feeling little solidarity with other working-class voters. His traditionalist feelings about gender roles show his lack of regard for egalitarianism. This man is not part of the feminized majority matrix, yet reiterates the complex relationship between gendered values and class—and the unexpected payoff of a feminized majority strategy for Democrats. This strategy appeals not only to men *with* feminized values, but also to nonfeminized men who would benefit from feminized majority policy. Their class and self-interests coincide with the political position of the feminized majority, even if they do not share feminized values. Such men are voting their economic interests rather than their values, and while not part of the feminized majority, may vote along with it.

This phenomenon similarly applies to some poor or working-class women whose values are more shaped by their conservative religion than their gender, but nonetheless vote Democratic. A 2005 Pew poll shows that there are millions of such women, whom the pollsters call "disadvantaged" or "socially conservative." Democrats.[10] These women are not part of the feminized majority either, because their religiously driven moral values overlap very little with feminized values. But they vote Democratic along with the feminized majority because of their economic interests. A feminized Democratic strategy appeals to men and women of lower classes who do not have feminized values but may vote progressively because of their class interests.

Most people vote both their values and their interests. Poor and working-class women tend to have feminized values of equality and cooperation that reinforce their economic interests and they are the core of the feminized majority. Upper-class women with feminized values who vote liberally are also an important part of the feminized majority because they vote their values rather than their class interests. Upper-class men are least likely to be part of or vote with the feminized majority, because (1) they tend not to hold feminized values, and (2) their economic interests lead them to vote Republican (the exceptions are highly educated men, often in the public sector, whose values are feminized and who vote these values rather than their class interests). Poor and working-class men are the most complex and divided because their economic interests and gender values point in opposite directions. Many with masculinized values vote with the feminized majority—despite not being part of it—due to their economic interests. Others, especially working men in unions, have developed feminized values of solidarity and equality and are part of the feminized majority, voting with it both for reasons of values and class interests.

The history of gendered values suggests again the importance of socialization in the creation of identity—as well as the complex interaction of values and interests in shaping how people vote. Although feminized values are historically associated with women, men can easily become part of the feminized majority. Democrats will benefit from understanding how men as well as women can hold feminized values, how values intersect with self-interest and class interests, and how both feminized values and working-class interests can shape a progressive policy that attracts both women and men.

CHAPTER SIX

How Democrats Can Win

The 2004 election showed that a values strategy works. John Kerry's loss also displayed the weaknesses of triangulation. In the aftermath of the race, poll after poll reflected the American public's belief that the Democratic Party had failed to portray John Kerry as a candidate of good moral character. Fifty-six percent of voters felt that Kerry "mostly says what people want to hear."[1] Voters felt a president should be "honest/trustworthy," a "strong leader," and have a "clear stand on issues." Not surprisingly, voters overwhelmingly felt Bush fit this profile better than Kerry.[2] And, of course, many voters felt Kerry was a "flip-flopper."

The 2004 election also shows what happens to Democrats when a candidate fails to inspire women voters. Whereas Clinton in 1996 and Gore in 2000 both won the popular vote with gender gaps of at least 10 percentage points, Kerry managed to inspire only a 7-point gap.[3] Many analysts suggest this difference may have cost him the election.[4]

Luckily for the Democrats, the failed Kerry campaign is an exception to the recent gender gap trend. Since the 1980s, the gender gap in elections at all levels has continued to widen. Unfortunately, the Democrats have yet to figure out what to do with this favorable data. Democratic political consultants are stuck in the paradigm of using gender gap research to better market their candidates *to women*.

To them, the research only provides a tool to attract more women to the party. Democrats treat women as an interest group, one of many subsets to be considered in their larger triangulation goals. Hence, they trot out the candidate's wife and children; use a female voiceover for certain campaign TV advertisements; or direct the candidate to stress so-called women's issues to female audiences.

The party needs to rethink this strategy. Gender gap data do more than show that women care about certain issues; it is the key to understanding the underlying *values* behind women's political opinions. Democrats need to get hip to these feminized values for two reasons: (1) millions of women will embrace a progressive agenda based on these values, and (2) feminized values have the potential to appeal to a much broader range of female *and* male voters. After all, it's not only progressive females who would benefit from the implementation of a feminized vision. The most important quality of feminized values is that they are universalistic and promote the well-being not just of women but of society as a whole.

Using the gender gap simply to try and gain more female votes leads to a political dead end. For example, in 1984, the Democratic Party looked at newly emerging gender gap research and, following the advice of the National Organization for Women, ran a female candidate for vice president. The Democrats thought that this action would motivate enough women to vote Democratic that the Walter Mondale/Geraldine Ferraro ticket would emerge victorious. This strategy confused simple biological femaleness with the much more complex issue of feminized values.

This is not to say that identity is irrelevant in women's vote choices. Voters certainly are influenced by feelings of solidarity or camaraderie with a candidate who looks like them. This is especially true for voters who have historically been oppressed. As Hillary Clinton and Barack Obama are discovering on the campaign trail, thousands of women and African Americans are rooting for them simply for the symbolic message their victory would send to the world. However, the Ferraro example shows that it will take Clinton more than her XX chromosomes to secure the widespread support of women.

Journalists often use Geraldine Ferraro as proof that pandering to women voters does not work, or even that the gender gap does not exist. In 2004 the *Washington Times*, recalling the 1984 election, editorialized that even though the Mondale-Ferraro team was "clobbered" by President Reagan, "the delusional feminists still divined a silver lining from the electoral shellacking by identifying a gender gap of six points: Men gave Mr. Reagan 62 percent of their vote, six more points than women."[5] Yet, the failure of the Democrats to win in 1984 does not make gender gap theories "delusional," it simply proves that the gender gap issue is complex, and that people who carry feminized values will not vote for a candidate solely because of her biological femaleness. Female candidates, like male candidates, need to convey feminized values clearly in order to win elections.

After Democrats attempted the Geraldine Ferraro strategy, Republicans looked at the gender gap research and came to a different conclusion: They could win the election by using sexual attraction. George H. W. Bush in 1988 said that he chose Dan Quayle as his running mate in order to win female voters. Although Quayle was not known as an advocate for women's issues, the Republicans bet that his good looks would be enough to attract women. Using the candidacy of JFK as their inspiration, the Bush campaign implored Quayle basically to flirt his way to victory.

What was missing from both of these strategies was any mention of *issues* that are important to women or any discussion of what values women held that led them to feel a certain way about issues. In 1992 Stanford researcher Felicia Pratto used the Bush-Quayle example to illustrate how political campaigns misunderstand women. Pratto found that women, regardless of their partisan identity, were more likely to support policies that were "hierarchy attenuating," or policies that challenged the dominant culture's position. "Women," Pratto says, "have a different stance from men toward one of the fundamental values that Americans, on average, like to hold dear, and that is social equality."[6]

The most important element to capture from this study, as well as from other research explaining the gender gap, is that women who are moving to the political left are casting their votes based on values, and these values are reflected through different political issues. All the research points to women's stronger feelings about equality, empathy, compassion, and diplomacy as the primary influence on how they vote.[7] Although Republicans have focused the moral values discussion only on evangelical Christian values, women view a range of political issues through their own moral lens. Women use their values to form opinions on the economy, war, and the environment. The Democratic Party needs to motivate these women— and men—who are part of the feminized majority. They need to adopt a platform based on *Together We Can.*

While many Democrats pay lip service to certain issues that interest the feminized majority, few Democrats have decisively embraced the major policy changes that the emerging majority demands. This reluctance can be attributed to two major forces in the Democratic Party that pull it in the opposite direction of the feminized base: its corporate fundraising base and its desire to capture masculinized voters. Both of these elements are by-products of the Reagan administration, which led America into a new era of corporate greed and aggressive militarism. The attacks on 11 September 2001 furthered this masculinization of politics. Today, candidates win elections by raking in huge corporate contributions and by engaging in verbal arm wrestling with their opponents to see who is the toughest. The corporate backers of the Democratic Party seek to shift sovereignty away from citizens in order to achieve their goals of higher profits. Naturally, they do not support policies of economic distribution and do not feel that helping America's most vulnerable citizens should be a high priority for the political parties. In this hypermasculinized, corporatist atmosphere, it is difficult to imagine Democrats promoting a platform of peace and equality.

This is not to say that corporations and masculinized voters agree on what the Democratic Party should look like; rather, masculinized and feminized voters both disdain corporate power or cronyism, as evidenced by a 2002 poll showing that 88 percent of Americans don't trust corporate executives and a 2005 poll indicating that 60 percent of Americans feel corporate America is doing a "fair" or "poor" job.[8] Yet, the masculinized values that privilege men in a capitalist society are the same values on which the corporate empire was built, and men are therefore more likely than women to support free market economic policies that benefit corporations.

Just as we should not confuse female voters with feminized voters, we cannot assume that male voters and masculinized voters are one and the same. A voter's biological sex does not necessarily coincide with his or her socially constructed ideas about gender. The challenge to the feminized majority strategy comes from the Democratic Party's desire to recapture masculine male voters who perceive the Democrats as weak. These masculinized men, or "alpha males" (as some journalists have dubbed them), represent a major tactical challenge to the feminized base strategy.

If the Democratic Party wants to win, it needs to recognize that its corporate fundraising base and its desire to capture white masculinized men are at odds with the feminized values driving the gender gap. By choosing corporations and machismo over constituents, the Democratic Party is missing an opportunity to galvanize the women and men of the feminized majority who yearn for a new era of American progressivism.

Toward Feminized Populism

The triangulation approach that worked so well for Democrats in the 1990s is not a viable long-term strategy for the party. Voters need to feel that their political party is in line with their values. Triangulation requires that candidates confuse voters about where they stand on the issues. As a consequence, voters become confused about what the party itself represents.

Evangelicals know where the Bush administration stands. President Bush assures Christians again and again that he shares their values and that he will not let them down. Evangelical voters feel they can trust him, that his motives are good, and that he means what he says. Few Democrats have this wholehearted trust in their candidates. The only thing the Democratic base knows for sure is that a Democrat in office—any Democrat—will be better than George W. Bush. But the Democratic Party needs more than to be seen as "the lesser evil." The party needs a revival, a way for people to vote Democratic with their hearts as well as their heads. Progressives need to fall in love with the Democratic Party again.

Values are the key to communicating with voters, and Democrats would be best served by adopting the values of the feminized majority. To motivate this growing base, Democrats should understand the roots of feminized values and push for policies reflecting these values. The feminized majority supports a *feminized populism*: a strong social welfare state; vigorous support for workers and working families; equal rights to redress the historical inequalities suffered by groups such as African Americans, Latinos, women, and GLBT Americans; a foreign policy based on cooperation and diplomacy; an environmental policy based on sustainability; and a democracy that is accountable to ordinary workers and citizens rather than to corporate and national security elites. But it's not enough to pursue these policies as progressives have in the past. Democrats also need to show a clear connection between their political positions and the values at the heart of these positions, making clear that this is a politics that is not just a collection of self serving needs of various Democratic interest groups. *A feminized populism is the policy agenda based on a feminized morality serving the entire society, weaving together universal feminized values of equality, cooperation, empathy, nonaggression, and community. It highlights the moral vision of a feminized world based on interdependence and caretaking.* When crafting policy, Democrats should always ask themselves: Does this plan reflect a *Together We Can* attitude?

Moving away from the current Democratic Party paradigm involves more than a change in message. It also requires a new relationship with the corporate interests that have played a huge role in the party for the last twenty-five years. This is the best way to show ordinary voters that Democrats are on their side. In the next chapter, we will outline how it is possible to run a campaign in a feminized way, relying more on average citizens than on corporate backers. Just as Republicans motivated evangelicals by running evangelical candidates, Democrats should support politicians who hold strong feminized values and who convey these values through their actions. Democratic candidates need to be unafraid to stand up to special interests, speak out against aggressive militarism, and fight for peace and justice. *Together We Can* extends beyond policy; it encompasses political strategy as well.

Three Steps for Victory in 2008 and Beyond

The Democrats need to do three specific things to mobilize the feminized majority and win in 2008 and beyond. The *first* is to run a campaign directed to the feminized majority. For years, while Republicans ran to their conservative religious base, Democrats have been running away from their own majoritarian constituency. The Republicans won by massively turning out their fundamentalist base voters. The Democrats lost because the feminized majority felt abandoned and were not inspired to go out and vote for a Bush-lite Democrat.

The first step involves rejecting the politics of triangulation and cultivating a different kind of "base" strategy. Bill Clinton was a master triangulator, and he used this strategy, along with his charisma, to win narrow victories. In the process, though, he abandoned the New Deal, consolidated the corporate regime, and helped undermine the identity of the party. Nobody was quite sure what the Democrats stood for after Clinton cut the ties to the party's New Deal moorings. The values of the New Democrats were murky, at best; people came to associate morality with Republicans rather than Democrats. The party itself lost any vision beyond that provided by Dick Morris and its other pollsters. They seemed to stand only for the narrow interests of their constituents and donors rather than to carrying forward a moral philosophy serving all. Republicans easily painted them as self-interested, bicoastal cultural elites, out of touch with the concerns and values of ordinary people.[9]

Much of the feminized majority stayed home and Democrats lost huge numbers of poor and working-class voters, the majority of them women. These feminized voters could have given the Democrats a comfortable winning margin. But they felt no connection to the triangulated, visionless, business-friendly group of New Democrats. The feminized majority constitutes most of the 100 million American voters who never entered a polling booth in the last thirty years. They thought there wasn't a dime's worth of difference between the parties.

Democrats must replace the politics of triangulation with a "base strategy" driven by values and speaking to the feminized majority. The feminized majority is much larger than the Christian conservative base of the

Republican Party. It is the majority of all voters in the country. And its only natural home in mainstream politics is the Democratic Party.

While cultivating a long-term relation with the feminized majority is the key to Democratic victory, it is not a "base strategy" in the traditional sense. Millions of members of the feminized majority are not registered Democrats. Some are registered Independents. Others are episodic voters or nonvoters. They will not necessarily line up with the Democrats on all issues—and until the Democrats change and pursue a robust feminized populist agenda, they will not become a loyal base.

George W. Bush was a gift to the Democrats in one sense. Six years of his rule was so devastating to the country that it finally mobilized disengaged Democrats in 2006 to vote Democrats into control of Congress. The feminized majority turned out from rage at Bush's masculinized values rather than any new values the Democrats were offering. As Republicans had showed earlier in its focus on Christian Right voters, you can inspire voters with a platform driven by strong values. The Republican losses in 2006 proved revulsion to values works too.

The Democratic Party has so deeply cut its ties to its New Deal history that it is clueless about how to develop its own "values politics." But all it needs to do is listen to its feminized majority constituency. The feminized majority is increasingly disenchanted with the hypermasculinized and hegemonic morality of Mars, and increasingly oriented toward the more egalitarian, empathic, and diplomatic morality of Venus. This makes clear the *second* step the Democrats must take to win: renounce the masculinized morality of the ruling corporate regime and assert the feminized alternative.

Asserting a new morality means forthrightly challenging the fundamentalist values of the Christian Right, the hypermasculinized morality of the warrior neoconservatives, and the ruling social Darwinist corporate values—and asserting a feminized populism. The feminized majority wants its own universalistic values brought into the public square and it will support the Democrats if they take up the challenge. This will take courage to enter "morality wars," align with feminized social movements, and take back values from Martian Republicans who speak of war, patriotism, and profits.[10] It is difficult to supplant the existing corporate morality with a more universalistic value system that speaks not just for the rich and powerful—and for the "me, me, me" of American individualism—but for larger social concerns. But because a strong values-driven feminized populism is the way to mobilize millions of Americans, and because feminized values are now majoritarian, it is a common-sense strategy for victory.

Despite some strong antiwar and populist rhetoric coming from Democratic 2008 candidates, this common sense is seeping in only slowly to the Democratic Party. It has too long been a corporate party in a corporate, hegemonic regime. It hardly knows how to disentangle itself and speak for a more universalistic moral vision. The party needs a catalyst to awaken and propel it in a truly new direction. That spark plug is not inside the party but outside it: the social movements within the feminized majority that are taking matters into their own hands. We have begun to see their influence in the form of MoveOn.org, progressive bloggers, and websites like DailyKos. These groups are carrying the universalistic values agenda from the feminized peace, women's, labor, and environmental movements to the Democratic Party.

Values politics never originate inside mainstream American parties. They always bubble up from the earth and the grass roots—and now the net roots. Who are these people and how do they express their values? They are the mobilized citizenry, the populist activists who are driven not by elections per se but by the intensity of their values. They are not shackled by corporate money, false patriotism, or political ambition. They act in their communities for local and global change based on feminized, populist values, and they are waiting to see if the Democrats will engage with them and follow their lead.[11] If they do so, in a critical *third* step, the Democrats will activate millions of disengaged members of the feminized Democratic base and bring them and feminized Independents into the voting booth. This is a winning strategy for the Democrats and the beginning of a new era in America.

CHAPTER SEVEN

Beyond Corporate Democrats

The creation of the Business Roundtable in 1972 hinted at the emergence of a new masculinized era in American politics. The Business Roundtable—which still exists—was initially composed of CEOs hoping to put more political power into the hands of an assertive business sector. Meeting regularly for lunch, the CEOs would discuss how the business community could increase its influence over government.[1] The Business Roundtable became, as Charles Derber put it, the "unofficial executive committee of the new establishment."[2] Following the group's inception, the politics of America for the next thirty-five years became increasingly corporatized.

The election of Ronald Reagan in 1980 finally gave the CEOs of the Business Roundtable the kind of president they had dreamed about. Reagan ran a government of, by, and for the corporations. Democratic Party leaders jumped on the new corporate bandwagon, alienating themselves from the rising feminized base. The corporatization of the Democratic Party is the single biggest hurdle to the feminized strategy for the party that we propose. The Democrats can neither become an enduring governing party nor enshrine a new progressive era until the party uncouples itself from big business. In this chapter, we describe when the Democratic Party became corporatized and suggest how it can begin to shed its identity as a corporate party and become the populist party of the new feminized majority.

Corporate Regimes and Gendered Values

The business community's chokehold on government is not new. Since the beginning of modern American politics, the government has swung like a pendulum—back and forth between corporate and progressive regimes. A *corporate regime* is created in a political system when the needs of corporations are given precedence over the needs of citizens.[3] During a corporate regime, the United States becomes a country "by and for" big business instead of the people. Both political parties get absorbed in the regime, embracing masculinized values and corporate policies. Feminized values are orphaned, with no political home.

The first corporate regime emerged during the Gilded Age of Rockefeller, Carnegie, and Morgan at the end of the nineteenth century. The second was the Roaring Twenties corporate regime, when big business again became king after the death of the first progressive regime (1901–1921) led by Teddy Roosevelt and Woodrow Wilson. In the 1930s, a second progressive regime emerged—a New Deal era spawned by the Great Depression when Franklin Roosevelt showed that Democrats can change the nation by embracing progressive and feminized values. As Democrats began abandoning these values in the late 1970s, and Republicans began to organize aggressively around corporate values and conservative Christian morality, the third corporate regime began under Reagan in 1980 and continued in full swing under George W. Bush.[4]

Figure 7.1 details some key differences between the two sets of underlying values that have steered corporate and progressive regimes.

If a corporation wants to secure profits for its shareholders, it cannot afford to view America through the lens

Feminized Values in Progressive Regimes	Masculinized Values in Corporate Regimes
Equality	Inequality
Compassion for others	Competition with others
Community	Winner-take-all individualism

Figure 7.1

of feminized values, because feminized morality requires softening inequality, competition, and aggression. In all three corporate regimes, government began to use corporate values as the basis for public policy. In all three eras, inequality and poverty grew, while profits soared. When masculinized corporate values, following the *Alone I Will* moral script, dictate how the government is run, and when both the Republican and Democratic parties embrace these values, the feminized majority suffers.

A Brief History of the Democratic Party in Corporate and Noncorporate U.S. Regimes

In the first corporate regime, Gilded Age entrepreneurs such as Rockefeller and Carnegie became icons, operating in the masculinized mode of Robber Barons but giving the appearance of America as a meritocracy. Masculinized discourse dominated America as the Robber Barons enshrined values of money, aggressive self-interest, and social Darwinism. Rockefeller and Morgan ran the government—and the big money, corporate lobbyists, and masculinized morality so familiar in our own era ensured that things stayed that way.[5]

While Republican presidents dominated the Gilded Age, this era created the first truly corporatized Democratic Party. The only Democratic president in the Gilded Age was Grover Cleveland, a Clinton-style reformer in the pocket of big business who openly expressed his masculinized values and corporate sympathies. Cleveland assured the Robber Barons that "no harm shall come to any business interest as the result of administrative policy so long as I am president."[6] Cleveland proved his masculine mettle by sending federal troops to attack workers during the famed 1894 Pullman strike. When workers pleaded for his assistance, Cleveland dismissively responded that "you might as well ask me to dissolve the federal government."[7]

A new populist movement responded to hypermasculinized corporate excess by trying to restrain capitalism through major social reform. The grassroots pressure was strong enough to get populist leader William Jennings Bryan nominated as the Democratic presidential candidate in 1896, but he was buried by the big money that the corporate titans threw at William McKinley. McKinley ended the populist threat, but when he was assassinated shortly after his reelection in 1901, Teddy Roosevelt ushered in a new progressive regime. The first corporate regime was history.

Roosevelt was a famed "rough rider" and imperialist leader with plenty of machismo and masculinized values, but he was forced to respond to grassroots anger at corporate greed. He embraced a public policy that was a synthesis of masculinized and feminized values. Feminized policies included the first national system to regulate corporations—a progressive triumph. But TR's masculinized values and corporate ties ensured that his regulatory system, while limiting the worst corporate excesses, would legitimize the corporate system and increase corporate profits.[8]

Woodrow Wilson, the Democrat who resurrected progressivism after his 1912 election, ruled with a Democratic version of this marriage of masculinized and feminized values. He used feminized Democratic ideals in discussing domestic reform and international democracy but allied himself with business interests and led the nation into a brutal, senseless war. The Democrats could not truly renounce the masculinized, corporatized identity they embraced in the Gilded Age.

Following the war came a period of hedonism and excess that we know as the Roaring Twenties. This ushered in another corporate regime, characterized by the advent of mass advertising and insatiable consumerism, and while women gained the freedom to smoke and wear short skirts, the era was heavily masculinized, dominated by corporate greed and financial mania. This second corporate regime also began the trend of "corporate paternalism."[9] Corporations such as the Ford Motor Company avoided union and government interference into their business affairs by promising to pay workers a living wage. These wages were enforced only by corporate self-regulation. This system makes workers seem like children receiving an allowance from a benevolent father. The Republican-led government stood behind the corporations in another expression of the masculine values that had ruled the first corporate regime and captured the Democratic Party of the Gilded Age.

The 1920s era of masculinized excess came to a grinding halt as the Great Depression hit America. In the regime that followed, the role of corporations shifted as an "activist federal government became the dominant institution."[10] The New Deal projects of President Roosevelt, during the New Deal second progressive era, brought major gains for worker rights, such as the Wagner Act and the Social Security Act, while also promoting a social welfare safety net particularly important for women, children, and families.[11] Although FDR was neither a populist nor

anticorporate, he did force big business to make conces-
sions to ordinary citizens. In doing so, FDR created a
new feminized paradigm for the Democratic Party. The
feminized narrative of *Together We Can* summarizes the
New Deal approach, and feminized values of equality
and cooperation gained greater ascendancy than ever
before in America. The Great Depression liberated the
Democratic Party from the straitjacket of masculinized
discourse and corporate values, and FDR put in place the
early foundations of a feminized social welfare order—but
only the beginnings.

The Third Corporate Regime and the New Corporatized Democrats

The second progressive era survived for another thirty-
five years. In the 1960s, a values revolution took feminized values way beyond the limits of the New Deal,
and it triggered a militant backlash led by corporations
and Christian conservatives, all under the rubric of the
Republican Party. Although the third corporate regime
was a long time coming, it crystallized with the election
of Ronald Reagan and still reigns.[12]

Today's corporate regime is different from those of the
past due to the increased power of American corporations
in a globalized economy. The scale, aggression, and power
of these corporations have helped create a hypermasculinized regime, a corporate regime on steroids. The yearly
profits of the largest global corporations exceed the GDPs
of many countries, and their political influence in the
global arena surpasses many countries. The U.S. government, as in the Gilded Era, has become a partner of large
corporations, but is now the junior partner.[13]

This newest hypermasculinized corporate regime
emerged under a Republican president, but the signature
of a corporate regime is its bipartisan nature, and the

current regime is no exception. Corporations pump staggering amounts of money into the election coffers of both political parties, ensuring that, no matter which party wins, the needs of big business are met.[14]

The Democrats' recent participation in corporate politics started in the first year of the newest corporate regime. In 1980, House Democrat Tony Coelho of California convinced the Democratic Party to adopt the Republican strategy of seeking political contributions from big business. This realization led to a shift in the relationship between the Democratic Party and big business, which had become strained because of the feminized policies of the New Deal. Political scientists Daniel Hellinger and Dennis R. Judd write about the effects of the Coelho strategy:

> Impressive signs of Democratic gains in fundraising lie in the comparisons of contributions to the congressional elections in 1984 and the off-year elections in 1986. In this two-year period, Democratic challengers and candidates for open seat races greatly increased their share of contributions from corporate, trade, and "nonconnected" PACs, while maintaining their near monopoly on labor PACs. Democratic candidates' share of corporate contributions rose from only 8 percent in 1984 to 28 percent in the 1986 off-year elections. In 1988, their share compared to contributions to Republicans rose to 27 percent.[15]

Although Coelho no longer calls the shots in the Democratic Party, his corporate fundraising strategies and alignment with masculinized corporate values have drastically changed the party. In the immediate years after the implementation of Coelho's ideas, politics in America changed dramatically. Ralph Nader offers a critical view of this era, writing, "The Democratic Party was fast losing its soul, morphing into the Republicans to form one corporate party feeding on the same corporate cash, but still sprouting two heads, each wearing different makeup."[16]

The election of Democratic president Bill Clinton, who had an emotive, feminized style but a masculinized "New Democratic" policy bent, reinforced the bipartisan nature of the current corporate regime, locking both parties into the masculinized values of corporate America.

The 1990s—even more so than the Reagan era—was a time of unprecedented corporate consolidation of power. Multiple corporate mergers, coupled with astonishing rates of economic inequality, recalled the Gilded Age of America—the first corporate regime. Although corporate executives replaced the Robber Barons, and President Clinton called the shots instead of President Cleveland, the corrupted democracy and social Darwinist thinking of the Gilded Age returned in full force.[17] America in the 1990s truly became the country by and for transnational corporations: a corpocracy. A corpocracy speaks the feminized language of democracy but imposes a masculinized corporate order unaccountable to the populace. Wisconsin senator Russell Feingold, a leader in campaign finance reform, observes, "We have devolved from a representative democracy to a corporate democracy in this country. This is not a system of 'one person, one vote' or 'one delegate, one vote,' but a system of '$1 million, one million votes.'"[18]

Bill Clinton's involvement in corporate politics began long before his presidential inauguration. After the embarrassing loss of Walter Mondale in 1984, a group of influential Southern Democrats came together to create a new strategy for the party, based on the goal of accepting corporate funding in every election. They called themselves the Democratic Leadership Council (DLC), and they vigorously promoted the remasculinization and corporatization of the Democrats. In 1990, Bill Clinton became the chair of the organization.

The DLC had the goal of moving the party away from "special interest groups"—women, minorities, and the poor—whose feminized demands countered the interests of the corporations willing to fund New Democratic campaigns. In order to marginalize those pushing for strong feminized policies, the DLC claimed that traditional Democrats were too focused on "class warfare," and that it is irrelevant to talk about the economy in industrial terms, like blue-collar and white-collar. The economy today, according to the DLC, is based on telecommunications, and a new "learning class" has developed. These "individualist new-economy workers will resist populism, reject Big Government, spurn unions, and abandon the social contracts of the New Deal and the Great Society."[19] In other words, the "New Democrats" are pursuing the serious business of shifting the Democratic Party from feminized to corporate values.

The true reason for the adoption of the DLC masculinized, anticlass rhetoric is that it soothingly paves the way for the Democrats to feel good about accepting corporate donations and pursuing corporate America's agenda. As political writer Thomas Frank says, "What politician in this success-worshipping country really wants to be the voice of poor people? Where is the soft money in that?"[20] He might have added, "Where's the money in the feminized majority?"

In 2000 Al From, the president of the DLC, proclaimed that someday soon, "We'll finally be able to proclaim that all Democrats are, indeed, New Democrats."[21] In each new session of Congress, the DLC gained the support of more and more freshmen members of Congress through membership in the New Democratic Network (NDN). The NDN defines itself as the "political action arm of the New Democrat Movement."[22] In the 103rd Congress, 16 percent of incoming freshmen joined the NDN. In the 104th session, 24 percent joined. In the 105th and 106th sessions, 60 then 70 percent of freshmen joined, respectively.[23] Bill Clinton, Joe Lieberman (before turning Independent), and former Democratic National Committee (DNC) chairman Terry McAuliffe, now a leading figure in Hillary Clinton's campaign, all consider themselves New Democrats. Although the DLC is waning, it thoroughly corporatized and masculinized the Democratic Party.

The Dean Campaign and the Beginnings of a Feminized Democratic Strategy

The Howard Dean campaign in 2004 broke with the DLC's corporatized approach. It personified the potential power of a new people–based Democratic Party strategy. Rooted in grassroots community action, the Internet, and "meetups," this new activist approach in the Democratic Party is a form of *Together We Can* politics. It is based on the feminized values of community and citizen cooperation rather than the top-down and masculinized corporate philosophy. While Dean lost his bid to be president, he is currently chairman of the Democratic National Committee, and his participatory, feminized model is beginning to infuse the Democratic Party.

Using the Internet as a fundraising tool, Dean created a base of 600,000 donors, most giving less than $100. Although Dean's platform was not revolutionary—he was not the most progressive or feminized candidate in the primary—he nevertheless challenged the established hierarchy within the party, and created an alternative for Democratic voters. Dean was eventually defeated, but he created a movement that changed electoral politics in a big way.

It is easy to call yourself a grassroots campaign when you don't have any money or support, and the Dean campaign certainly did not have much of either. Based in a 1,000-square-foot office above a Burlington, Vermont, pub, the Dean campaign was an underdog to say the least. Having no support from the Democratic establishment, the Dean campaign was forced to move in a different direction—away from big donors and toward everyday

Americans. Campaign manager Joe Trippi talks about how the campaign stumbled upon the idea to fundraise in a new way.

> Early on, we had a meeting to figure out how we were going to bring the Dean campaign around. ... We could look for help from political action committees, of course, but that was the antithesis of the Dean campaign—like asking the oil companies for money to create alternative fuels. The other campaigns were going the $2,000 chicken dinner route, but we knew there simply weren't enough rich people for us to hit up for money. So maybe we could appeal to regular Americans, get two million of them to donate a hundred dollars each.[24]

The key to the new fundraising style was decentralization, and the best tool for decentralization is the Internet. The Dean campaign website used a link to meetup.com, a site that facilitated meetings for people with similar interests, such as sports teams or animals, or a political candidate. Meetup.com allowed hundreds of thousands of grassroots Dean supporters to mobilize all over the country, without being coordinated or controlled by the campaign. This decentralized populism is an expression of feminized values, because it follows the script of *Together We Can* and relies on cooperation and community at the grass roots. It represents a revolutionary kind of presidential campaign, made possible by new forms of technology that put a measure of power in the hands of the people. The Internet is perfect for this kind of movement because, as Trippi says, "its roots in the open-source ARPAnet, its hacker culture, and its decentralized, scattered architecture make it difficult for big, establishment candidates, companies and media to gain control of it."[25]

Meetup.com and the rise of "meetups" that constituted the base of the campaign show the feminized nature of this politics. Meetups are meetings in people's kitchens or living rooms to raise money and build common visions and projects. Meetups are a tangible expression of the politics of *Together We Can*, and the Dean campaign rested on its volunteers taking this feminized moral narrative very seriously. The feminized value of equality is built into the meetup because everyone is a volunteer with an equal voice. The feminized value of community becomes central because if the meetup does not create a community spirit, it will not succeed. And meetups have to embrace a feminized cooperative ethos because if volunteers do not work together in true collaboration, the campaign will fail.

Beyond this feminized method, Dean's campaign hinted at a new feminized populist vision: the need for Democrats to shift power from corporations to ordinary people. Dean did not offer a systemic critique of the corporate system, but he did suggest that democracy had been eroded by the huge infusion of corporate money and lobbyists into Washington. Dean's manifesto, "You Have the Power," was a feminized and populist argument that workers and ordinary citizens had the capacity to return power to the people and strip corporations of their political stranglehold over both political parties.[26] His fundraising strategies were one means of beginning that process, liberating the Democratic Party from the control by corporate donors and proving that ordinary citizens could provide a powerful and fairer political substitute.

Dean subtly infused feminized values into both the substance and methods of the Democratic Party. Feminized themes of equality, cooperation, and community undergirded his critique of corporate power and drove his vision of a new Democratic politics fueled by citizen activism. Had he been more assertive of his critique of corporate hegemony—and more forceful in contrasting feminized with corporate morality—he would have mobilized a much greater sector of the feminized majority. A vast majority of Americans believe, according to polls reviewed in Chapter 4, that corporations have too much power, and Dean might have won had he been more explicit about his populism as a moral agenda that could end corporate rule and serve the rising feminized majority.

But Dean's new feminized campaign vision and strategy, while insufficiently critical of corporate power, gained traction rapidly. The first feminized campaign strategy was working. By essentially handing over the campaign to average Americans, Dean began raising more money and gaining more poll support than any other Democratic candidate. He was far and away the frontrunner in most primary states, including the crucial states of Iowa and New Hampshire. He was doing so well, in fact, that the campaign decided to opt out of federal matching funds, which would have placed a cap on total fundraising. This decision was made by posting an online referendum and asking Dean supporters to make the final decision—80 percent voted to opt out.

As Dean moved up in the polls, his fundraising tactics became more creatively feminized. In July 2003, a Dean blogger noted that Dick Cheney was hosting a $2,000-a-plate fund-raising lunch. The supporter came up with the idea of asking people to donate $25 or $50 to watch a streaming video of Howard Dean eating a turkey sandwich. Whereas the Cheney luncheon raised $250,000 from 125 people, the Dean "luncheon" raised $500,000 from 9,700 people.[27]

The new feminized politics did not sit well with corporate Democrats or corporate America. The Dean campaign felt the effects of angering media conglomerates and their corporate sponsors. The media drastically turned on Dean, and many feel this led to the campaign's demise. The best example of Dean's negative publicity came on the night of the Iowa caucuses, when Dean gave a passionate speech to screaming supporters about how his campaign would continue after coming in third place. People at the event were enthralled by how Dean was able to use the Iowa loss as a motivational tool for his fans. The media, on the other hand, was overjoyed at how silly they could make certain portions of the speech sound by filtering out the roar of the crowd. A clip of Dean's speech was replayed almost 700 times on national news networks and given as evidence that Dean was too angry and unstable to be president.[28] The strategy worked.

If anyone had a right to be disheartened by the outcome of the Dean campaign, it was Joe Trippi. Yet, Trippi is optimistic about the future, and understands that the Dean campaign was the first step in a drastically new direction in politics.

> Dean for America is a sneak preview of coming attractions—the interplay between these new technologies and our old institutions. The end result will be massive communities completely redefining our politics, our commerce, our government, and the entire public fabric of our culture. For ten years, it has been the dawn of this movement. Now it has arrived. For years, we've seen the Internet as a revolution in business or in culture. But what we are seeing—at its core—is a political phenomenon, a *democratic movement* that proceeds from our civic lives and naturally spills over into the music we hear, the clothes we buy, the causes we support.[29]

But the real change is not the high-tech revolution of the Internet but the moral revolution from corporate to feminized politics. Kerry's loss to Bush in the 2004 presidential elections showed that the Democratic Party had lost its moral moorings and its own feminized base. In the third corporate regime, Democrats came to believe that corporate values were Democratic values and that corporations were their most important constituency. But the Democrats can win and change the country only if they pursue a politics of values that stirs the soul of the rising feminized majority.

Democrats, Moms, and the New Politics of Feminized Values

Feminized values voters are guided by principle. If the Democratic Party wants to win, it needs to pursue a feminized platform of peace and equality that clearly rejects the corporate agenda and reflects the values of the feminized majority. The majority of Americans feel that big business is morally corrupt and is eroding democracy and our core values. The Dean campaign showed that, by running a campaign that does not rely on corporations, the Democratic Party will find supporters in unexpected places.

Feminized values and corporate values are irreconcilable. Feminized base voters, who support equality, compassion, and community, reject the dog-eat-dog capitalism played out by corporations. The Democratic Party has attempted to straddle the line between these two forces for two decades and has ended up bewildered and lost. By letting go of its corporate values, and embracing the worldview of the feminized base, the Democrats will gain broad support from the American electorate.

Although Democrats view many groups of conservative voters as a lost cause, pushing a feminized, anticorporate agenda could have the effect of transcending party lines and ideology, bringing together broad groups of citizens who feel that their government is being hijacked by the corporate elite.

If the Left and Right can come together to promote populist goals, it is worth examining what issues truly are preventing a feminized-driven realignment. Studies prove that as the Democratic Party has adopted a conservative economic agenda, moral issues have gained considerable salience in elections. Due to Republicans' brilliant political maneuvering, the term *moral values* is now synonymous with *conservative values*. Political writer Jeff Taylor questions the idea that moral values arc conscrvativcs' tcrritory, and uscs thc cxamplc of thc impact moral issues had on the campaign of Ralph Nader in 2004. Exit polls showed that 3 percent of voters who listed "moral values" as the most important issue in the campaign cast their vote for Nader. Taylor writes that "among the issue blocs, [Nader] received by far the most support from this group, and it was disproportionately high compared to his total vote percentage."[30] As ironic as it may seem, given the religious right's domination of the moral values debate, Nader's voting base turned out to be those most concerned with America's morals.

The Nader campaign again raises the question of why the Democratic Party has allowed Republicans to dominate the moral values discussion, and why the word "values" has become synonymous with "evangelical Christian values." Anna Greenberg expands on this, showing how Democrats can frame other issues using morality:

> Rather than accept the Right's narrow definition of values, progressives should acknowledge the challenges parents face dealing with their kids' sexuality and peer pressure around drugs and alcohol in an environment overrun with sex and violence on television, the Internet, and video games. Democrats and progressives should begin to talk about these concerns in simple language and should not shy away from taking progressive positions that are consistent with what moms value.[31]

In speaking of "what moms value," Greenberg hints at the broader agenda of the feminized majority. It includes a forceful moral assault on corporate power and inequality, and the promotion of policies serving the needs of working moms—and working dads. It also involves a moral denunciation of a foreign policy based on violence that violates moms' values and has made both moms and dads more insecure.

Furthermore, as values-driven Democrats aim to reach the feminized majority, they should recognize that they will touch a nerve among evangelical Christians. The 2006 midterm elections showed evangelicals and progressives coming together in disdain for government corruption. According to the *Washington Post*, in the 2004 House races, Republicans received 74 percent of the evangelical vote, and Democrats received 25 percent. In 2006, 70 percent of evangelicals voted for Republicans, and 28 percent voted for Democrats. Roberta Combs, chairman of the Christian Coalition, attributes the change to corruption among Republicans. Reverend Richard Land, head of the Southern Baptist Convention, says evangelicals are "disgusted that Republicans came to Washington and failed to behave any better than Democrats once they got their snouts in the trough."[32] Corporate corruption is a moral issue to voters. By adopting a feminized base strategy, and therefore changing their relationship with corporate donors, Democrats will be able to mobilize supporters—who may not agree on every issue—and move America into a new era of progressivism.

Americans, more than anything else, want a government by and for the people. If the Democrats want to win elections, they need to rethink their corporate allegiances, and pursue a message resonating with the values of those they are trying to motivate. Feminized values are not in sync with corporate values, and we now have a feminized majority, not a corporate one. By pursuing a feminized base platform, the Democrats will gain the support of the new American majority who feel that their government is in the hands of a corrupt elite that is sabotaging the values and well-being of most moms and millions of dads in the name of traditional morality. The rising feminized majority wants and deserves something better.

Chapter Eight

Attracting Men

"The Invasion of the Alpha-Male Democrat," a recent *New York Times* headline blared, in response to the proliferation of new Democratic congressmen with ultramasculine biographies. In recruiting Democrats to run for Congress in 2006, the party establishment sought men with a certain character. John Lapp of the Democratic Congressional Campaign Committee says, "We went to C.I.A. agents, F.B.I. agents, N.F.L. quarterbacks, sheriffs, Iraq War vets. These are red-blooded Americans who are tough."[1]

In a post-9/11 world, the Democrats reason, Americans are looking for politicians to protect them, who are physically and mentally tough; with the physique to win in a bar fight and aggression enough to make terrorists sorry that they were ever born. To the Democratic Party, the 2006 midterm elections were certainly not the time to push politicians such as Dennis Kucinich, a vegan, who would certainly lose in a bar fight and spends a lot of time talking about peace and spirituality. Strategist James Carville explained the situation, "The fact that the party has come across as less—I don't want to say less masculine—but certainly less aggressive than Republicans, is true."[2] Carville, in a roundabout way, admitted the party's true strategy for the 2006 midterm elections: *Be more masculine to win back men.*

In this chapter, reflecting on the "alpha-male" strategy Democrats devised in 2006, we consider how a feminized

127

Democratic Party can attract men. Feminized values obviously attract more women than men, but Democrats need men to win. Millions of men hold feminized values, but not enough to ensure robust Democratic victories, especially in conservative states. The key to victory is substance rather than symbolism. But we show that masculinized symbols, particularly in Red States, can help Democrats promote a feminized populist agenda that attracts both women and men.

Men, Alpha-Male Symbols, and a Feminized Democratic Platform

In 2006 the Democratic Party, unsurprisingly, once again targeted voters by presenting them with candidates who look like them. Faced with the problem of lagging male support, they needed masculine candidates. And the strategy worked—sort of. While "alpha-male" candidates won many tough races, their victories, like most Democratic victories of the past fifteen years, came as a result of the gender gap. For example, Jim Webb, one of the candidates profiled in the *New York Times* article, received 55 percent of the female vote, and only 45 percent of the male vote.[3] Men with masculine biographies returned Congress to the Democratic fold by appealing heavily to women as well as attracting enough men to win.

If women are the majority voting masculine men into office, then do these candidates truly represent the alpha-male profile? In biology, the term *alpha male* simply refers to the animal that others follow and defer to. In human society, the term refers more generally to a man who is on top of the power ladder. To the Democrats and the *New York Times*, however, the term refers to men with "carefully cultivated masculinity" who "are throwbacks to the era when tough-guy Democrats were urban ethnic politicians like Dan Rostenkowski and Tip O'Neill."[4] While the

2006 candidates could biologically be the alpha males, did they carry an alpha-male value system? No matter how much these candidates love sports, or how many pushups they can do, they appeal to hypermasculinized voters only by having *masculinized values*. And, as we shall show, because their values were feminized, they lost many conservative "macho" men but won a majority of women and a significant minority of men who might have otherwise voted Republican.

John Tester of Montana provides an interesting case study of the relationship between a male's masculine biography and his value system. The *New York Times* describes Tester as a "husky Montana farmer with a buzz cut" who is part of the new "tough-guy caucus" in the Senate. The fact that Senator Tester's background involves manual labor is often mentioned as proof of his masculinity. Plus, he's a gun owner. He even says on his website that he "will stand up to anyone—Republican or Democrat—who wants to take away Montanans gun rights."[5] Yet, does being a gun owner and having a "husky" build make someone an alpha-male politician?

Tester, after all, won his seat because he appealed to 52 percent of female Montana voters.[6] Were these women attracted to his masculine biography, which was supposed to be a tool to bring back male voters, or was there something else that drew the women to him? More importantly, why did a majority of men support his opponent, Conrad Burns? After all, the Democratic Party candidate had a buzz cut and was much huskier than Burns. Tester fared much, much better than the previous Democrat who ran against Burns in 2000—Schweitzer garnered only 39 percent of the male vote—but still captured a minority of 48 percent of men. How much brawnier does a Democratic candidate need to be to win a majority of male voters?

If the Democratic Party truly wants to attract ultra-masculine white males, there is plenty of research that shows what they need to do. Anna Greenberg traces the loss of white males from the Democratic Party. Starting in 1964, men's support for the Democrats dropped dramatically. She attributes this to the policies of Lyndon Johnson, who promoted a series of "Great Society" social programs, aimed at alleviating poverty and lifting up the most oppressed in America. While men understood and identified with previous state efforts at economic intervention, such as the New Deal, they felt Johnson's program created an unnecessary burden for average Americans. She writes, "With these shifts, white men's stake in government decreased. White men became particularly hostile to welfare programs for the poor, which were no longer justified as universal social insurance."[7]

Since the Johnson presidency, men have become increasingly distrustful of government. Seventy-four percent of white men agree with the statement, "The government is wasteful and inefficient," compared with 64 percent of women. Further, 66 percent of men "favor smaller government with fewer services to larger government with many services," but only 51 percent of women do. Overall, Greenberg writes, "there is no sense of a stake in the collective goal of making people's lives better."[8] Therefore, if John Tester represents the return of the alpha male to the Democratic Party, then he should have run on a platform of small government, and the elimination of "wasteful" social welfare programs. He should have denounced Great Society–type programs as being elitist and exclusionary. His rhetoric would have focused on the masculinized values of self-reliance, efficiency, and individualism.

In reality, John Tester's platform drastically differs from this alpha-male profile. While he is progun, he is also prochoice and pro–stem-cell research. More important than these typical male and female issues, however, is the language Tester uses when discussing his position on all issues. He does not support alpha-male issues because he does not have alpha-male values.

Instead, his core values are feminized. The Tester platform denounced corporate power and supported feminized populism. "Money has far too much influence in government today," he writes. Tester promises that he will "stand up to big insurance companies and support a health care plan that makes health care affordable to all Montanans." He also will "stand up to big drug companies and support legislation allowing the government to negotiate lower drug prices for Medicare Part D."[9] In a newspaper editorial, he writes, "I see regular folks being forgotten in favor of special interests," and that "backroom deals are cut, not on the basis of what's best for the average Montanan or American, but on who can write the biggest campaign check." Energy companies "reap record profits while the rest of America struggles to pay their bills." He even promises to ask a Montana judge to conduct an ethics audit of his office every year.

Another theme in the Tester platform is community. When discussing his support for stem-cell research, Tester writes, "Montana values mean doing everything you can to help a sick neighbor." He supports raising the minimum wage, saying that workers deserve pay that is "fair" and "livable." Most importantly, Congress could learn a few lessons from the Big Sky State. "Montanans are ready for a change that will bring Montana values back to the halls of Congress. Values like family, faith, hard work and community."[10] These values do not sound like alpha-male capitalist values.

We can agree that Tester embodies many masculine traits—his husky build, his love for hunting, and his previous job as a farmer. However, Tester also holds many feminized values, such as compassion and a commitment to equality and community that translated politically into a moderate feminized populism. The Tester campaign shows the complexities of marketing a candidate using gender. It demonstrates that: (1) a person's value system is shaped by many factors besides his or her gender, and (2) a person's understanding of gender is shaped by factors other than his or her value system. Tester certainly would not concede that his compassion comes from his desire to reject his masculinity. Nor would he agree that, because he is a man, he must act less compassionate. Although he holds values into which women are traditionally socialized, and even though women may respond to these values by voting for him, it is unnecessary to ask Tester to espouse these values *as* gendered values.

The implications for Democratic Party political strategy are clear. Promoting candidates in Red States who carry aspects of alpha-male symbolism can actually mobilize the feminized base, both female and male, as long as the candidates themselves promote a strong feminized values agenda, such as universal health care, support for working people, the return of government to the people, and international diplomacy. Paradoxically, the alpha-male symbolism may help legitimize Red State candidates who oppose a politics based on alpha-male values. And such candidates, while they won in 2006 by winning a robust majority of women's votes, also succeeded in bringing more men into the Democratic fold.

Red State Democrats, such as Tester, won mainly because of their populist agenda. Even in conservative states, a feminized populism produces results. It attracts a majority of women because it speaks both to their values and to their economic and social needs. It also attracts a significant minority of men, who respond to the populist economic substance buttressed by the masculinized symbolism.

In Chapter 5, we pointed out that a feminized politics can appeal to men either because (1) they hold feminized values, or (2) a feminized populist agenda best serves their economic interests. Working-class men who have masculine values and are thus not part of the feminized majority may still be attracted to a feminized

Democratic Party that forcefully speaks to their interests: better wages, better health care, and better education and job training. Feminized Democrats appeal to nonfeminized men mainly because they speak to their pressing economic and social needs. But the alpha-male symbolism can help because it allows these men to believe that their Democratic votes do not compromise their masculinity. Even for men with feminized values, especially in states such as Montana or Virginia, the masculinized symbolism may make it easier to vote Democratic.

Two caveats: First, the alpha-male symbolism can turn off the feminized majority in Blue States, where feminized symbolism is more likely to mobilize the base. Second, the symbolism in both Red and Blue states must be used strategically to promote rather than undercut feminized policies. The feminized majority represents an increasingly robust *national* majority of voters. The prime aim of the Democratic Party should be to align its policies with those values. Symbolism is important, and masculinized symbolism in Montana and other conservative states can promote feminized politics in surprising ways. But what counts ultimately is the policy.

Militarism: The Largest Chasm Between Masculinized and Feminized Voters

Tester's platform is not an alpha-male platform. The purpose of running candidates like Tester is obviously to convey a certain image, not revolutionize Democratic policy. In fact, nowhere in the *New York Times* article do DNC strategists even *mention* policy. Rather, they push ambiguous ideals like toughness, red-bloodedness, and aggressiveness. But, what do these words even mean, and where is this strategy coming from? Why do the Democrats want so urgently to adopt this toughness strategy now?

The answer clearly relates to 9/11. While toughness, red-bloodedness, and aggressiveness are certainly gendered terms, they are also closely associated with the military and with patriotism. The alpha-male strategy, therefore, is a symbolic gesture signifying that the Democratic Party supports a strong military. By running candidates like Tester, the Democrats were trying to straddle the line between alpha-male voters and the feminized base. But, will this strategy work in the long run?

Research shows that the Democrats are running serious political risks if they overstate alpha-male symbolism and fail to attack U.S. militarism. Some of the largest ideological gaps between feminized values voters and alpha-male voters emerge in questions about military force, with the feminized majority increasingly outraged about the Iraq War and about the Bush administration's militarism. Democrats will not persuade the new feminized majority to support the party if they embrace an imperial, alpha-male approach to U.S. foreign policy.

Leaders of both mainstream political parties have long collaborated to promote the view of America as a bastion of freedom and the military as an essential instrument to protect and spread American ideals. The Democratic Party remains wedded to this paradigm, despite the antiwar feelings of its base. The 2004 Democratic Party platform begins a section about the need for a larger military with the following: "We need a new military to meet the new threats of the 21st Century. Today's American military is the best in the world, but tomorrow's military must be even better. It must be stronger, faster, better armed, and never again stretched so thin."[11]

Democratic leaders and the Democratic Party remain committed to U.S. hegemony. John Kerry, Bill Clinton, Hillary Clinton, and Barack Obama critique the Iraq War as a "mistake" but support the notion that the United States must remain the strongest military force in the world in order to advance a hegemonic foreign policy that secures America's place as the dominant global economic and military power—the "leader of the free world." No major Democratic leader has openly challenged the imperial motives driving many U.S. interventions and wars, such as the rapacious interest in oil and oil prices that helped drive the U.S. invasion of Iraq both in the 1991 Gulf War and in 2003. The Democrats remain tied to the long, bipartisan policy of "immoral morality," where immoral and illegal wars and regime changes are moralized as spreading liberty and defending Americans and the world against terrorism.[12]

Despite broad public fear about terrorist attacks, the Democratic Party leadership will not attract the feminized majority if it continues to embrace a hegemonic, hypermilitarized foreign policy. The feminized majority wants resources redirected from the military to American social needs at home. It wants Pentagon money cut so that we can improve our deteriorating public schools and health care system. It wants to stop demolishing homes in Baghdad and start rebuilding homes in New Orleans. And it wants to "support the troops" by bringing them home from Iraq and not sending them off into other hegemonic adventures.[13]

But the Democratic Party has not completely miscalculated politically in embracing alpha-male symbolism. The feminized majority is disenchanted with U.S. militarism but not yet with the military. Although a huge majority of Americans oppose the Iraq War and Bush's foreign policy, the vast majority of Americans also support and trust the military. One survey found that 72 percent of Americans trust military officers to tell the truth.[14] Another poll asked respondents to rate the prestige of different occupations. Eighty-one percent of respondents rated "military officer" as having "very great prestige" or "considerable prestige."[15]

The feminized majority also remains conflicted about American hegemony. It supports the United Nations, international law, and a diplomatic and cooperative approach to foreign policy. But when a feminized politician like Dennis Kucinich proposes radically cutting defense spending and ending America's domineering position, even the feminized majority doesn't respond uniformly favorably. Only 18 percent of Americans agree with Kucinich that the military budget is too large; in fact, 25 percent think it should be increased.[16] While the feminized majority thinks very differently about war than masculinized voters, and while they have different moral standards about acceptable codes of conduct during war, they still cannot be classified as pacifistic, nor have they resolved their increasingly conflicted views about hegemony and the U.S. military.

This reflects the long history of elites from both parties defining American global power and dominance as not just moral but a moral obligation—to spread freedom.[17] Such "immoral morality" is accompanied by a manipulation of patriotism in which anyone who opposes American wars is "swift-boated" as a traitor who is endangering American troops and betraying America itself. This "betrayal narrative"—a form of permanent McCarthyism—has long silenced dissenters and turned peace activists, such as the young John Kerry, into leaders capable of calling a war a "mistake" but afraid to cast doubt on the legitimacy or morality of American power and intentions.[18] The betrayal narrative—and the concept of patriotism that infuses it, as well as the repression that can be exercised in its name—has kept even many within the feminized majority confused and fearful about questioning the U.S. military or America's global military dominance.

In this context, the most progressive political strategy for the Democratic Party is to pursue a clearer antihegemonic policy that engages the yearning of the feminized majority for peace and global cooperation. It may help in Red States to run candidates such as Webb or Tester, whose alpha-male symbolism helps legitimize a critique of a hypermilitarized U.S. foreign policy; however, feminized values win elections for Democrats, whether they are espoused by John Tester or Barbara Boxer. Although Tester's masculinized image and biography may have helped in Montana, it was ultimately his platform that won his election.

It may seem counterintuitive, but Democrats will *not* lose crucial feminized support by running candidates in Red States who symbolize masculinity and military strength, as long as the candidates clearly pursue an antiwar, less hegemonic agenda based on feminized values. That remains the most important thing Democrats can do to win and transform the nation, whether it is cloaked in feminized or masculinized symbols. As antihegemonic social movements get stronger at the grass roots, the Democrats will be forced to respond with their own more vigorous critique of hegemony—and a reasoned, alternative vision of America's place as one of many nations seeking a new order of international law and cooperation.

CHAPTER NINE

Edwards, Obama, Kucinich, and Feminized Male Courage

Hillary Clinton announced her intention to run for president, a landmark moment in American history, with a web message titled "I'm In." At this writing, Clinton is the leading candidate for the Democratic nomination and has a strong chance of becoming president. Her presidency would mark the coming of age of the new feminized majority.

A woman president, of course, is not the same thing as a feminized president. In the next chapter, we shall see that Clinton is a pathbreaking but imperfect carrier of the feminized agenda. President Franklin Roosevelt carried out a more progressive feminized policy revolution than we are likely to see from a President Hillary Clinton. But Clinton could bring to the White House something unique as a president who is of and by—if not entirely for—the new feminized majority.

Yet by the time you read this book, the voters may have chosen another Democratic candidate. As of this writing in late 2007, we can play out a few possible scenarios with several of the other Democratic candidates. We start with an analysis of Edwards and Obama, the two "top-tier" male candidates, and assess their qualities and views on issues through the lens of feminized analysis. We also include a portrait of Dennis Kucinich, a long shot for the Democratic nomination, but certainly the most feminized candidate in the race. In the next chapter, we move on to a more extended analysis of Clinton—not only because she leads in the polls and is America's first serious female presidential candidate, but also because she embodies many telling contradictions that help illuminate the complexity of feminized politics.

Prefacing this discussion of the Democrats, we need to emphasize that all the major Republican candidates in 2008 ran hypermasculinized campaigns. Rudy Giuliani ran a testosterone-infused campaign based almost entirely on terrorism and his toughness to fight to the last man to win what some of his aides, such as neoconservative Norman Podhoretz, called "World War IV." Giuliani's reputation was based almost entirely on his carefully crafted image during 9/11, as a heroic, can-do male who symbolized the resolve of the nation to crush the terrorist barbarians threatening Western civilization.

This supermasculinized vision of international politics was the Republican brand throughout the 2008 campaign, permeating the candidacies of John McCain, Mitt Romney, and Mike Huckabee. McCain ran a campaign that Bush had not been manly enough, and McCain drew male throngs of soldiers, veterans, and other masculinized men, especially in the South, who resonated to his extremely tough talk. Romney was slightly less macho in his polished business style, but no less masculinized in his emphasis on building American military dominance and crushing the insurgents in Iraq and the global Islamic fascists. Mike Huckabee had a feminized style but a hypermasculinized policy on terrorism, immigration, abortion, guns, and gay rights.

The supermasculinization of 2008 Republican politics spilled over from foreign policy into economics and social values. Romney proclaimed that Republicans stood for a tripod of strength: military, economic, and family. He pledged to be the man who had what it took to deliver in all three areas. Giuliani focused on military power but, like all the Republicans, pushed for intensifying even further than Bush a hypermasculinized capitalism that would cut feminized safety nets and spur self-sufficiency, the classic masculinized value in America. He would cut taxes and government, the Republican domestic mantra that played to the traditional values of masculinized self-reliance and mocked feminized social services as breeding dependency and weakness. In the context of this super-masculinized Republican politics, the feminized politics that we show below among Democratic candidates is striking, even where the differences were more stylistic than issue-based.

John Edwards, Barack Obama, and Dennis Kucinich: Feminized Males?

Edwards, Obama, and Kucinich demonstrate that men can become successful feminized leaders with potential to change the Democratic Party. Of the "top-tier" candidates, John Edwards is the most feminized candidate on substantive policies and in his personal passion and empathy. While both Clinton and Obama remained vague on substance, Edwards immediately came out swinging on issues, with specific feminized proposals. The man who in 2004 had run against the "two Americas"—the division of the nation into rich and poor—broadened his focus and fleshed out a serious, detailed agenda in 2007–2008, turning himself into a feminized populist.

Edwards proclaims "a moral crisis in corporate America." He argues that corporate greed and corporate globalization were creating a new class of working poor, as corporations downsized, outsourced workers, and busted their unions. In a North Carolina factory town, Edwards drew on his own roots as a son of a mill worker to speak from the heart about the agony of poverty, the struggle of working families, and the moral urgency of a fairer and more egalitarian America. Both his personal emotion and his intense focus on equality—backed by specific proposals to tax businesses that outsource, democratize corporations, build labor rights into trade agreements, and redistribute income—makes Edwards a surprising voice for feminized populism.

Edwards emotionally speaks about the importance of unions, which epitomize the master feminized narrative: *Together We Can.* Edwards is personal about unions and workers' struggles:

> We don't believe it's right that a man or woman could be fired from the job for trying to organize a union in the workplace, so that working people actually have a voice. And this is something I take very personally. My mother and father have health care today because of the unions. My younger brother is a card-carrying member of IBEW; he and his family have health care today because of the union. We need real labor law reform in this country.[1]

This personalization is essential to feminized politics. It links Edwards's own family experience to a central moral issue. Edwards talks about his own personal activism to build the labor movement:

> Since the 2004 election, I have been all over this country organizing workers into unions, because if we want to strengthen the middle class, if we want to lift millions of Americans out of poverty, one of the most critical pieces is to grow the union movement.... But, whoever is elected president of the United States, the one thing you can take to the bank: as long as I'm alive and breathing, I will walk picket lines with you, I'll help you organize, and I will stand with you.[2]

Not surprisingly, Edwards began attracting endorsements from major unions like the steelworkers, mine workers, carpenters, and transportation workers. This reflects not just his empathy and policies supporting unions, workers, and the poor, but his position on many other core feminized issues.

Edwards became the first major candidate to offer a specific program for universal health care.

> My universal health care plan would require employers to cover all their employees or pay into a fund that covers the cracks in the health care system. . . . It's complete mental health care, there's coverage for chronic care; coverage for preventative care; coverage for long-term care. We subsidize health insurance premiums for low-income and middle-income families. And the last responsible party besides the employers and the government are individuals. Everyone in America will be required by law to be covered by this health care plan.[3]

Universal health care is at the heart of a feminized domestic agenda. It involves vital human rights essential to the well-being of every family and requires the empathy that is the spiritual foundation of feminized politics. By mandating health care for all and by emphasizing themes of children's health, prevention, long-term care, and mental health parity, Edwards strongly embraces the core feminized value of equality.

Edwards also takes strong positions on environmental sustainability and climate change, on rebuilding New Orleans after Katrina—calling the government's response "the shaming of America"—and on civil rights and women's rights, saying that "racial inequality is the heart and soul of my campaign" and that he was "a better advocate for women than Hillary Clinton." These rhetorical flourishes vividly express feminized values of empathy, equality, morality, and stewardship. No other mainstream candidate, except perhaps Obama, put such an overtly personal and moral floodlight on these feminized issues.

In foreign policy, especially on Iraq, Edwards takes an unapologetic feminized position. He openly proclaimed that the "biggest professional mistake in his career" was his vote for the war in Iraq; his willingness to apologize embodied a feminized sign of strength. And he argues against keeping forces in Iraq and for immediately withdrawing approximately 50,000 troops in the fall of 2007, leading many to compare his forceful antiwar stance to Howard Dean's position in 2004. It's worth noting that Joe Trippi, Dean's leading campaign strategist, signed on with Edwards, and brought the same participatory—online and grassroots—feminized approach to the Edwards campaign that marked the Dean campaign.

As a feminized antiwar candidate, Edwards strongly critiques the Democratic Congress for not using its constitutional authority to withhold funding and bring the Iraq War to an end. Although he has not explicitly opposed American global power or militarism, he opposes all nuclear weapons and is critical of the war on terrorism as a cover for American interventionism. "But what this global war on terror bumper sticker political slogan" really is, Edwards says, is just a bumper sticker. "It's all it's ever been. It was intended . . . for Bush to use it to justify everything he does. The ongoing war in Iraq, Guantánamo, Abu Ghraib, spying on Americans, torture, none of those things are OK. They are not the United States of America."[4] Edwards not only reflects the feminized value of peace but also comes as close to a feminized critique of American hegemony as any mainstream presidential candidate has offered.

Because Edwards took such strong feminized positions, he did not attract the money that big donors, lobbyists, and corporations poured into Clinton's and Obama's campaigns. This hurt his campaign, not because the feminized majority did not agree with his views but because the media ranks the seriousness of a candidate by the money he or she is able to raise—and because money determines how much advertising and television exposure a candidate gets. Money also affects perceptions of electability, and even many in the feminized majority who love Edwards for his positions on the issues feared that he might not be able to win and gravitated to either Clinton or Obama.

* * *

Barack Obama emerged as the most serious rival to Clinton through most of the 2007 campaign, leading Edwards consistently in the national polls although trailing Clinton. Obama is also a feminized candidate, but in different ways than Edwards. Obama's feminization derives principally from symbolic and stylistic calls for a "new politics" rooted in feminized values of diversity, equality, and community. Obama understands these values because of his upbringing. He is biracial, and spent his childhood living in Hawaii and Indonesia. Obama's diverse life experiences made it difficult for him to find his place in the world, until he decided he simply belonged to the "community of humanity."[5]

Obama skillfully built on his identity to create a new politics resonating powerfully to the feminized master narrative of *Together We Can.* Just as Obama feels he can bring black and white Americans together for a common cause, his principal campaign theme involves overcoming the bitter, polarizing partisanship of recent years and emphasizing, in a feminized spirit, the "values that bind us together." In the introduction to his best-selling book, *The Audacity of Hope,* Obama writes: "The ideals at the core of the American experience, and the values that bind us together despite our differences, remain alive in the hearts and minds of most Americans.... I offer personal reflections on those values and ideals that have led me to public life, and my own best assessment of the ways we can ground our politics in the notion of a common good."[6]

Here is Obama's feminized philosophy in a nutshell. He highlights the importance of values in his own life and in the nation's politics. He emphasizes that there is a "common good" or universal set of values that can bring Americans together. He stresses change and the movement from self-interested partisanship to a feminized politics of the common good.

Obama emphatically argues that values must drive politics. Obama offers a gentle feminized critique of the Democratic and progressive shift from a moral to an interest group politics: "I am not suggesting that every progressive suddenly latch on to religious terminology. I am suggesting that perhaps if we progressives shed some of our own biases, we might recognize the values that both religious and secular people share when it comes to the moral and material direction of our country. We need to take faith seriously not simply to block the religious right but to engage all persons of faith in the larger project of American renewal."[7]

Obama sees the values uniting America as commitment to equality, the rule of law, human rights, and cooperation and community—all core feminized values rooted in the Declaration of Independence, America's most feminized founding document: "We gather to affirm the greatness of our nation, not because of the height of our skyscrapers, or the power of our military, or the size of our economy. Our pride is based on a very simple premise, summed up in a declaration made over 200 years ago, 'We hold these truths to be self-evident, that all men are created equal. That they are endowed by their Creator with certain inalienable rights. That among these are life, liberty and the pursuit of happiness.'"[8]

This is feminized politics in an American idiom. He is highlighting the feminized values of equality and human rights as core American ideals. He is rejecting masculinized symbols of greatness: skyscrapers, military power, and economic growth. With great skill, Obama subtly feminizes an aggressively masculinized American history.

Obama is markedly feminized in his critique of the self-interested, greedy "old politics" of partisanship. "It is such partisanship that has turned Americans off. What is needed is a broad majority who are reengaged and who see their own self-interest as inextricably linked to the interest of others."[9] Here, the feminized Obama challenges the historic, masculinized American dream of looking out for oneself. Obama seeks to move America from narrow "self-interest" (the masculinized narrative of *Alone I Will*) to a concept of shared interest with others (the feminized narrative of *Together We Can*, which Obama often cites as "Yes, We Can").

Obama's feminized personality adds symbolic credibility to his political discourse. He is gentle, inclusive, and empathic. He also is willing to show vulnerability, especially about his own biracial biography. He wrote of the inner tension he experienced as a young African American community organizer struggling with his own "white blood":

> As I imagined myself following Malcolm X's call, one line in his book stayed with me. He spoke of his wish that the white blood that ran through him, there by an act of violence, might somehow be expunged. I knew that, for Malcolm, that wish would never be incidental. I knew as well that traveling down the road to self-respect my own white blood would never recede into mere abstraction. I was left to wonder what else I would be severing if and when I left my mother at some uncharted border.[10]

Like Edwards, Obama is willing to open up tender and painful areas of his inner life. This tendency combines with an idealism and hopefulness to resonate a feminized sensibility. Obama is also a cunning basketball player who makes time for games while campaigning, so he has not compromised his masculinity, even as he openly displays so many attractive feminized qualities.

On issues, Obama is far less feminized than in his style and rhetoric. At this writing, he has been vague in his policies, saying that campaigning is more about broad principles and trust rather than specific programmatic agendas, making it difficult to characterize how feminized a president he would be. Yet enough in his record shows that, although he tilts toward feminized policy, he melds masculinized and feminized values in a way that is not by itself likely to create major feminized or populist change.

This is most evident in his foreign policy, a contradictory blend of feminized and masculinized approaches. Obama rejected the Iraq War from the beginning, a feminized centerpiece of his 2008 campaign that he used to differentiate himself from both Clinton and Edwards. He flatly calls Iraq "the biggest foreign policy disaster of our time,"[11] and endorses the feminized guiding principle that war is a last resort and must be consistent with international law.

Obama garnered attention for saying that he would talk in his first year as president with the presidents of Iran and Syria and "that it is a disgrace that we have not spoken with them."[12] Other candidates, such as Clinton and Christopher Dodd, hammered him for "inexperience" and naïveté. But Obama strengthened his credentials as a feminized candidate committed to diplomacy rather than violence. Like other mainstream candidates, Obama never questions American hegemony or the country's moral claims to the world. But with a feminized lilt, he often speaks of strengthening international law, human rights, and global community, all through dialogue and diplomacy. And beneath the surface there is a hint that the United States is abusing its power. "Never," Obama proclaimed, "has the U.S. possessed so much power and never has the U.S. had so little influence to lead."[13]

A masculinized Obama, though, crops up just as frequently in his foreign policy pronouncements. In 2007 he said that he would not hesitate to attack terrorists inside Pakistan without that country's permission—a more hawkish position than even George W. Bush had taken. His Democratic rivals called it another sign of inexperience and confusion. Supporting preemptive strikes inside a nation that is your ally is certainly a masculinized position clashing with his feminized antiwar posture.

Moreover, Obama opposed the Iraq War partly because he saw it draining military resources from the war against Osama bin Laden and al-Qaeda. The comment about striking terrorists inside Pakistan was symptomatic of his aggressive support of the war on terrorism. Feminized values acknowledge the need for self-defense, but Obama goes further and supports more troops and money for a global masculinized hunt against terrorists. He proposes "growing" the military to chase terrorists down: "Our most complex military challenge will involve putting boots on the ground in the ungoverned or hostile regions where terrorists thrive.... That should mean growing the size of our armed forces to maintain reasonable rotation schedules, keeping our troops properly equipped, and training them in the skills they'll need to succeed in increasingly complex and difficult missions."[14]

Increasing the already enormous U.S. military contradicts Obama's feminized focus on diplomacy, while "putting boots on the ground" is a tacit endorsement of new interventions wherever a U.S. president sees a threat. By taking this tack, Obama commits himself to an overly simplistic militarized approach to the terrorism issue, one that distorts the largely political nature of the problem and the feminized view of the need to change U.S. foreign policy to deal with it. Buying into the idea of a "war"—rather than a political solution combined with globally coordinated police action against terrorism—will not appeal to the feminized majority.

Obama straddles the masculinized/feminized divide in foreign policy. As the 2008 campaign unfolds, he increasingly emphasizes the importance of soft power—diplomacy, international law, and cooperation—in the war on terrorism. He continues to flesh out his feminized position that American security comes only with greater security of other nations, that human rights and U.S. security are indivisible, and that abandoning human rights in the name of the war on terror is dangerous and antithetical to the principles of the United States. Obama melds masculinized and feminized values in his foreign policy ideas, appealing to the values of the feminized majority without repudiating military power as his ultimate foreign policy card.

On domestic issues, Obama is a modest feminized reformer, proposing incremental changes that stand little chance of changing our masculinized capitalist order. He supports expansion of health care, but seeks neither to mandate universal care nor to end the corporate takeover of medicine. He supports labor and environmental clauses in trade agreements, proposes to end tax breaks for corporations that outsource jobs abroad, and would reward corporations that practice social responsibility, all loosely feminized positions. But there is little hint of a populist sensibility that rallies voters around serious challenges to corporate power.

One exception is Obama's strong support for reforming campaign finance laws, curbing corporate lobbyists, and cleaning up the horrific corruption in Washington. This reflects Obama's focus on values and underlies his constant claim to be a "messenger of change." Efforts to end corporate control of government—and return America to its citizens—are central to feminized populism. But one looks in vain for Obama's specific policies that could achieve anything close to such a deep feminized change. Obama's problem is not the "inexperience" that his rivals constantly berate him for. It is his failure to provide the feminized substance—the real change in policy—that would put flesh on the bones of his eloquent feminized rhetoric and symbolism. This harms Obama's prospects with activist Democrats and the broader feminized majority.

* * *

The one 2008 candidate who advocates systemic change is Ohio congressman Dennis Kucinich. Kucinich is a *radical* feminized politician. While he is not a "top-tier" candidate, for reasons we discuss shortly, he illustrates where a truly feminized politics could eventually lead. As another feminized leftist, Tom Hayden, famously said, "Today's radicalism is tomorrow's common sense."

Kucinich says he will abolish the Pentagon and create a new "Department of Peace." Kucinich's radical feminized values are most visible in his rejection of war as a moral principle. Kucinich pulls no punches: "I see peace as being the central issue and concern of our time. I see all of the issues that we're speaking about connected to peace, with peace at the center. And in a Kucinich administration, we would begin with an understanding of the centrality of peace to life in the United States and to life on our planet. We would begin with policies which reject war as an instrument of policy."[15] No other candidate expresses such a radically feminized language and vision.

Kucinich's commitment to peace is rooted in a passionately held moral philosophy: "Our nation's waiting for a grand vision which sees the world as one, which understands that the world is interconnected and interdependent, and that it is indeed our job to heal this planet, to bring this planet together as one people."[16]

Kucinich is calling the feminized majority to take seriously its own most basic principles. The feminized values of interdependence and connection become the foundation of a new world community, embodied in the shared humanity of all peoples.

> The neo-conservative doctrine of recent decades "Peace through Strength" has been an unmitigated disaster, weakening our national defense, weakening our military, weakening our economy and weakening our standing in the world.

> The Kucinich doctrine of Strength through Peace ... means the end to resource wars, the end of wars for control of oil. It means no more attempts to subvert the governments of other countries. It means the end of assassination as U.S. policy. It means working to affirm the human rights of people all over the world by the United States standing for human rights.[17]

His passion to "heal the planet" by creating a world community at peace with itself and the environment is an unabashed expression of the feminized ethos of caring and stewardship.

Kucinich's values directly contradict principles of empire and the masculinized notion of the war on terrorism. At a 2007 South Carolina presidential debate, the moderator asked Kucinich why he is the only candidate who does not raise his hand when asked whether he believes "there is such a thing as a global war on terror." Kucinich responded, "Because the fact of the matter is that the global war on terror has been a pretext for aggressive war."[18] Kucinich is the only candidate who rejects the "war on terrorism" as a masculinized instrument of American empire, a "ticket to ride" for the hawks and neoconservatives running the nation's foreign policy.

Kucinich "loves America" but his radical feminized values lead him to reject completely American militarism, starting with his call for immediate withdrawal from Iraq. His "first act as president" would be to go to the United Nations and get a resolution to endorse complete American withdrawal in ninety days. During a 2007 presidential candidates' debate, he demanded the impeachment of our leaders, specifically Vice President Cheney, for leading us into this unconstitutional war:

> This is a pocket copy of the Constitution, which I carry with me, because I took an oath to defend the Constitution. This country was taken into war based on lies about weapons of mass destruction and al-Qaeda's role

with respect to Iraq, which there wasn't one at the time we went in. I want to state that Mr. Cheney must be held accountable. He is already ginning up a cause for war against Iran. Now, we have to stand for this Constitution. We have to protect and defend this Constitution. And this vice president violated this Constitution. So I think that while my friends on this stage may not be ready to take this stand, the American people should know that there's at least one person running for president who wants to reconnect America with its highest principles.[19]

Kucinich's call for impeachment is based on a moral commitment to international law and the Constitution utterly inconsistent with American empire and hegemony. "This is about our Constitution," he says, "It is about our adherence to international law. I'll move to have the U.S. join the International Criminal Court. It is absolutely necessary that all of us be held to the same standards that we would want everyone else in the world held to."[20]

Kucinich attacks the moral conceit that America cannot be subjected to the same standards as other nations. This notion of a true equality of nations—all subject to the same international laws, rights, and responsibilities—challenges American hegemony on pure feminized principles that Kucinich finds in America's founding documents. This allows Kucinich to reject the entire masculinized structure of American hegemony in the name of love for America's deepest moral values.

These same radical feminized values lead Kucinich to repudiate America's current capitalist system and to call for a transformation of the nation's social order. Kucinich argues that the collusion between corporations and government is dangerous.

We need a new relationship between our government and corporate America, an arms-length relationship, so that our elected leaders are capable of independently affirming and safeguarding the public interest. Just as our founders understood the need for separation of church and state, we need to institutionalize the separation of corporations and the state. This begins with government taking the responsibility to establish the conditions under which corporations can do business in the United States, including the establishment of a federal corporate charter that describes and clearly delineates corporate rights and responsibilities.[21]

Kucinich, a relentless critic of corporate power, has moral, even spiritual, passion: "Commerce must be guided by moral principles. This is something that I understand from my own spiritual training. Workers' rights are human rights, and there is a moral arc that we have to follow in all of our commerce. It's time for a president who understood the concerns of workers, who stood for workers."[22] In this statement, the outlines of a radical feminized populism are clear. Corporate power violates the human rights of all workers and citizens. It undermines the core feminized values of equality, community, and democracy. Kucinich takes populism beyond impersonal Marxist notions of scientific materialism often expressed by the left. His approach is very personal, and thus very feminized. He grew up in a poor working-class community, and talks of how his life experiences shaped his political priorities:

When I was growing up in Cleveland, the oldest of 7 children, my parents never owned a home. We lived in 21 different places by the time I was 17, including a couple cars, and sometimes we were the only Caucasian family in neighborhoods of color. And because of that experience in growing up in the inner city, I became attuned to the concerns that people have about jobs, about health care, about education, about housing.

And so, when I became mayor of Cleveland, I was determined to unite the community, to unite whites and blacks and all people of color, and to create conditions where we truly address the social and economic needs of the people.

> Because of my life experience and because of my public
> life experience, I have the ability to lead this nation and
> to bring all people together and to lift up the cause of this
> nation so that we once again become a nation that comes
> from the heart and reconnect with our optimism to really
> create a nation that we can all be proud of.[23]

This call to "become a nation that comes from the heart"
is pure feminized imagery that links Kucinich's childhood
in the inner city to a passion for feminized transformation. He wants a world that can "bring all people together"
and "truly address the social and economic needs of the
people."

Unlike other candidates, Kucinich links this soaring
feminized rhetoric to a huge array of specific and systemic
feminized populist policies. These range from breaking
up corporate monopolies in oil, agriculture, and banking
to creating a single-payer government-based universal
health system. Kucinich would immediately pull America
out of NAFTA and the World Trade Organization, and he
opposes all "free trade" agreements. He wants to "restore
our manufacturing jobs. Save our family farms. Create
full employment programs, create new jobs by rebuilding
our cities and schools."[24] He supports "positive" human
rights to health care, education, a job, a living wage,
decent housing, and child care and elder care. He wants
full-blown public financing of campaigns that will take
the big money out of politics and return government to
the people. "I'm the only candidate for president," says
Kucinich, "who will take this country away from fear, from
war, and tax giveaways, and use America's peace dividend
for guaranteed health care for all. Take the profit out of
health care. I'm the only one who will stop privatization
of Social Security and bring the retirement age back to
age sixty-five." "This is a grassroots campaign," Kucinich
boasts, "to take back America for the people. Join me, for
your cities, your towns, your farms, and your campuses.
Join me, and let's take back America."[25]

With such powerful and eloquent feminized politics, why did Kucinich not lead the Democratic pack and get the enthusiastic backing of the feminized majority? Four reasons: First, his positions made it impossible for him to get the corporate funding required for a major campaign. Without personal wealth of his own, it was impossible to get the television exposure and advertising that would make him known. Most Americans have probably not heard of Dennis Kucinich.

Second, his positions undermined his credibility in the mainstream media, who treat him as a loony maverick and rarely report anything about him. This reflects the media's addiction to the money game as the Holy Grail of credibility and electability. It is a sign of the media's own corporate bias, rooted in the reality that corporations own most newspapers and will not countenance such overt challenges to the corporate order. To support or even write respectfully about Kucinich could endanger a reporter's or editor's credibility, and maybe his or her job.

Third, Kucinich threatens the mainstream leadership of the Democratic Party in Washington, which is still tied to the corporate regime. Feminized populism of the Kucinich stripe is a barely disguised assault on the Democratic Establishment, and exposes the party's capitulation to the corporations that fund it. Kucinich calls for a feminized revolution in the Democratic Party as well as in America itself. Not surprisingly, the party leaders—and his mainstream rivals—join corporations and the media in treating him as a pariah.

Fourth, Kucinich is, in fact, more radicalized than much of the feminized majority. His values and positions resonate strongly with many progressive activists and millions of ordinary feminized voters. Voters from a blue-collar Ohio district repeatedly reelected him to Congress by large margins. And he was mayor of Cleveland. Nobody can claim Kucinich does not understand the American heartland, nor that working Americans—the Ohio bus drivers, factory workers, clerks, and nurses' aides who keep reelecting him—do not understand and love him.

But his anticapitalism and pacifism, while based on feminized values shared by the majority, will sound quirky or extremist to many citizens. As he says, he *is* different. Both his style and issue positions are well outside the boundaries of "respectability" that corporate America and the mass media create and enforce. As a short, vegetarian, overtly spiritual pacifist, his image clashes with the masculinized "strong leader" Americans still associate with power. His radicalism makes it easy to portray him as a coward, a communist, or a traitor.

The feminized majority also gets trapped in perceptions of electability created by the mass media and opinion makers, who have marginalized Kucinich. Even those supporting his views regard him as unelectable. This self-reinforcing cycle has long served elite interests and continues to make even voters who agree with Kucinich doubt that there are enough others like themselves who might actually represent the new majority. But Kucinich plays a prophetic role in moving feminized values into the limelight. He will not be elected president. But he is awakening the feminized majority to the radical implications of its own morality. If Cleveland voters can love this man, the growing feminized majority nationwide may one day conclude that his radical vision of healing and transformation grows organically out of their own feminized values.

CHAPTER TEN

Hillary Clinton and the Hope of a Feminized Future

It is difficult to understate the symbolic implications of a Hillary Clinton presidency. To elect a woman as president of the United States would be an enormous breakthrough. Women have been elected leaders in Britain, India, Israel, and many other nations. But the United States is the world's hegemonic power and the planet's supreme model of masculinized capitalism. This makes a female president seem almost miraculous. Tens of millions of American women—and millions of men also—are waiting to see if they can tell their daughters that "you can be anything you want, even president of the United States."

Identity plays a key factor in politics and a major role in values-driven movements. The feminized majority will become visible as the new commanding force in American politics when a woman becomes president. That is why even women and men who are far more progressive and feminized than Clinton are emotionally engaged in her quest. And it is why so many Republicans hate Clinton despite her centrist leanings; she symbolically threatens America's masculinized worldview.

In this chapter, we offer an overview of the strengths and weaknesses of Clinton as the messenger of the feminized majority. She is less feminized in 2008 than Dennis Kucinich, John Edwards, and Barack Obama. Clinton has a more corporate agenda and a history of supporting the Iraqi War and U.S. militarism. As we show later, she, like her husband, triangulates as a politician rather than acts in tune with populist anger and the hopes of the feminized majority.

This is not to say that Edwards and Obama consistently support feminized values. All of the "mainstream" candidates embody many contradictions, both in their policies and their campaign strategies. When John Edwards announced that his campaign would accept public financing, few political pundits believed his explanation about "taking a principled stand" against the big money pervading politics—it's hard to accept that Edwards would have made the same decision had he surpassed Clinton and Obama in fundraising totals. *The Nation*, in fact, called his decision an act of "political pragmatism," a label that reflects Americans' general cynicism about the motives of politicians.[1] None of the leading candidates have escaped criticism about whose interests they represent, and our critique of some of Clinton's ideas should not suggest that Edwards or Obama would be the perfect feminized candidate.

We consider three profiles of Hillary Clinton—only one of them is feminized. Nonetheless, Clinton symbolizes the feminized ascendancy as no other politician can. In Clinton's case, this goes beyond her biology. Clinton's strong record of supporting "working families" represents the feminized rather than Christian conservative vision of family values. As the daughter of a preacher, she believes in a values-driven politics and sees issues through the moral prism of the feminized majority. No candidate speaks with the rhetoric of *Together We Can* with quite the same lilt as Hillary Clinton.

Although we disagree with some of Clinton's ideas and strategies, we recognize the challenges she faces as the first woman running for president. She must negotiate different parts of her identity in ways that none of the male candidates can understand, and is forced to make political decisions with her gender in mind. This is especially true because she is a Democrat. Clinton knows, for example, that voters might react differently to a Democrat's antiwar campaign strategy depending on the gender of the candidate. As many reporters have pointed out, what voters see as empathy in Edwards or Obama may be seen as weakness or oversensitivity in Clinton. Clinton, much more than Edwards or Obama, takes a risk by standing up for the feminized values of peace and diplomacy. In fact, because of her gender and party affiliation, Clinton takes a risk every time she supports progressive policy. Her campaign strategy surely takes these challenges into account. Many feminist voters know this, and therefore dwell less on what Clinton says or does to get elected. They just want a woman with certain obvious feminized perspectives to finally occupy the Oval Office.

As a female Democrat, Clinton faced special challenges in the light of the supermasculinized Republican message discussed at the beginning of the last chapter. The hyper-masculinized campaigns launched by Giuliani, Romney, and McCain played on public fears of terrorism, pulling out the traditional Republican card of military strength and patriotism after 9/11. But recognizing that a women was likely to be the Democratic nominee, Republicans salivated about the prospect of tarring Clinton and her Democratic Party with an image of feminine weakness, out of step with the mind-set necessary in the age of terrorism and "Islamo-fascism."

We keep these gender-linked manipulations in mind in discussing and sometimes criticizing Hillary Clinton's positions. Despite our critiques, we believe that both because she is a woman and because of her position on certain key issues, Hillary will open a window to a new feminized politics. If Clinton is elected, she will not transform American capitalism or end the country's global military adventures. But much as John F. Kennedy, also a centrist, created space for progressive social movements of the 1960s, her presidency will could allow the rising feminized majority to express itself. This will require the continued rise of new grassroots bloggers, movements, and organizations—such as MoveOn.org and other environmental, labor, and peace groups—pushing and pulling the Democratic Party under Clinton's leadership to transform the country.

Village Clinton

Long before the 2008 campaign season began, Clinton had already won over many feminized voters because of her pivotal book *It Takes a Village* (1996). The book, whose title brilliantly evokes *Together We Can* politics, offers a powerful feminized message not just for raising children but also for remaking America. Clinton is not just a woman, she's also a carrier of feminized values about family, work, and community.

Village Clinton, the profile she presents most visibly in talking to Democrats, is strongly feminized, in both rhetoric and substance. In *It Takes a Village,* Clinton shows her feminized colors. It goes beyond typical "women's issues" like affirmative action, education, and health care. Clinton urges Americans to help end poverty, create affordable housing, improve unemployment insurance, increase the minimum wage, and confront prejudice.

She advocates gender equity for the good of all society, arguing that feminized values are for everyone, not just women. She writes, "Children learn what they see. When they see their fathers cooking dinner or changing the baby's diaper, they'll grow up knowing that caregiving is a human trait, rather than a female one. When they see their mothers changing tires or changing fuses, they'll accept troubleshooting as a human quality, rather than a male one. We should be mindful of the messages we send them as well as the behavior we demonstrate."[2] What's best for children, says Clinton, is for parents to be open-minded and transcend traditional gender roles to create a more humane, caring, and egalitarian society.

The last chapters of her book, particularly, raise the issue of corporate power, the main hurdle to creating a feminized America. While we show shortly Clinton's limitations in this area, she concludes her book with a hint of a new feminized populism. In the chapter titled "Every Business Is a Family Business," Clinton turns her attention to the dangers of "unchecked corporate power." She writes: "While we want to encourage competition and innovation—hallmarks of American capitalism—we need to be aware of the individual and social costs of business decisions. In every era, society must strike the right balance between the freedom businesses need to compete for a market share and to make profits and the preservation of family and community values."[3] One problem, she says, is that "too many companies, especially large ones, are driven more and more narrowly by the need to ensure that investors get good quarterly returns and to justify executives' high salaries."[4] Clinton also points out the growing chasm between the wages of executives and those of average workers.

What America needs, Clinton writes, are more "community-minded companies." As examples, she praises companies that have worked with the government to create business practices that take workers, consumers, and the environment into account. When discussing the future of the economy, she quotes Harvard Business School professor Rosabeth Moss Kanter, who writes, "Companies will understand the need to rebuild the corporation and create a sense of community again. The ones that do that will be the winners in the next stage of the competition."[5]

By framing the book around "the Village" vision, and ending the book with these populist themes, Clinton makes a strong pitch to the feminized majority. While her approach to business relies on corporations voluntarily changing their practices, a position far from the robust populist platform that America needs, she implicitly calls for a check on unrestrained capitalism and advocates for the rights of citizens over the desire for higher profits. Clinton's call for corporate restraint is a message the feminized majority wants to hear from her. Village Clinton offers a glimpse of a feminized populism that speaks to the values and needs of the feminized majority.

In 1996, Clinton famously argued, "We are all responsible for ensuring that children are raised in a nation that doesn't just talk about family values but acts in ways that values families."[6] She's proud of her long record supporting policies that "value families," which she argues is the litmus test of commitment to family values. In 1993, she called for universal health care. It was the most important progressive initiative of her husband's presidency. Health care for all lies at the heart of feminized family values, because no family can prosper without staying healthy, and universal care expresses the egalitarian and empathic spirit at the heart of feminized culture. The 46 million Americans without any health care symbolize the larger crisis of affordable health care facing all Americans, and Hillary made it her signature issue.

Attacked by conservatives as "an unprecedented intrusion into the federal economy," her plan died.[7] Now, fifteen years later, Americans are yearning for a health care system based on the universalistic values of the Clinton health care plan.[8] On 17 September 2007, Clinton announced a new model of a universal health care plan that would require every American to have health care. It retains private insurers, and allows people who like their current plans to have them, but requires that people without a plan either buy into a subsidized private plan or a government plan. Pledging $110 billion for her "Health Care Reform Plan," Clinton said "It is time to provide affordable health care to every American. And I intend to be the president that finally accomplishes this for our country."[9]

Clinton's plan is not the most robust feminized model of universal care, since it leaves the door wide open for private insurers who can cherry pick the healthier patients. The universal, single-payer program that Michael Moore proposes in his wildly popular documentary, *Sicko* (2007), is far more closely aligned with the needs and values of the feminized majority. But while this hints at Clinton's limits as a feminized populist, she is offering a major step forward to meet one of the most basic needs of the feminized majority and all of America.

Meanwhile, Clinton's track record speaks to a broader feminized resolve to "value families." She has introduced a raft of legislation to support working families: The Family and Medical Leave Act gives parents paid time off when their children or other family members are ill. She has also introduced a bill to double the child tax credit and expand it to cover more poor families; a bill to support additional unemployment insurance for parents who are laid off from work; a bill to raise the federal minimum wage to $7; and a bill to make it easier for unions to organize. She also consistently supports the agenda of major labor unions; opposes Bush's tax cuts for the rich; and opposes cuts in social programs for welfare, child support, and student loans. These positions help explain why Clinton's strongest base is liberal voters, along with poor and working-class women. In a July 2007 poll, 66 percent of liberal voters had a favorable view of Clinton, her highest among any category of voters. Fifty-one percent of women making less than $50,000 also had a favorable opinion and only 24 percent a negative view.[10]

Feminized voters identify with Village Clinton: the steadfast advocate for families and workers. Americans are looking for a candidate who will protect their jobs, Social Security, and health care. The feminized majority wants a president on their side, not an ally to the rich and powerful. They want politicians to tell them that *Together We Can*. If the Democrats want to turn things around, Clinton's "Village" vision and her agenda of a feminized family values is a place to start.

Hegemonic Clinton

Along with a feminized Village Clinton exists a masculinized Clinton. The masculinized Clinton supports corporate capitalism and a muscular military to maintain U.S. global hegemony. The militarized "Hegemonic Clinton" poses a huge problem for the feminized majority and erodes her authenticity as a feminized candidate. Nowhere has this come out more strongly than in her position on the Iraq War.

In the second Democratic presidential primary debate in 2007, the top three contenders sparred over who would best lead America into the era of peace and community that voters so desperately yearn for. Edwards, Obama, and Clinton disagreed about who supported the war in Iraq, when, and based on what information. The candidate receiving the most attention for her Iraq position was Clinton.

Clinton was at the forefront of the Iraq debate due to her reluctance to divulge her motivations for initially supporting the war and her refusal to apologize for this support. This puts her in a different position from her two main opponents. Obama, though an Illinois state senator when the war was authorized, nevertheless opposed it from the start. Edwards, who, like Clinton, voted to authorize the use of force in Iraq, has since apologized vigorously. "It wasn't just the weapons of mass destruction I was wrong about," Edwards announced on *Meet the Press* in February 2007. "It's become absolutely clear—and I'm very critical of myself for this—become absolutely clear, looking back, that I should not have given the president this authority."[11] Clinton, on the other hand, minimized the importance of an explicit apology, telling voters at a Dover, New Hampshire, campaign event, "If the most important thing to any of you is choosing someone who did not cast that vote or has said his vote was a mistake, then there are others to choose from."[12]

Clinton's reluctance to take as firm a position on Iraq as Edwards or Obama personifies Hegemonic Clinton, who supports a huge American military establishment, a globalized U.S. military dominance, and a militarized War on Terror. The Hegemonic Clinton is tough and un-yielding.

Hegemonic Clinton sees vacillation or acknowledgment of error as weakness, a trait shared by masculinized leaders, such as George W. Bush, who fear compromising their tough posture. Rather than firmly stating that the war in Iraq is unwinnable, that the occupation breeds more anti-American terrorists, and that the elected officials who authorized the war were wrong, Clinton maintains a tough, promilitary demeanor and refuses to move too far toward the antiwar left. She is unwilling to create a perception that she is pulling America back from its globally dominant position, a reflection of her consistent commitment to U.S. hegemony.

However, as we mentioned earlier, many view Clinton's reluctance to disavow her Iraq vote as less a sign of her foreign policy position than of the unique challenges she faces as a female candidate. Pundits often advise female candidates to be cautious when speaking out against militarism. What seems like compassion on Edwards's part could be perceived on Clinton's part as a woman's inability to stand up under pressure. In their essay "Hillary's War," Jeff Gerth and Don Van Natta Jr. argue that Clinton's vote was part of her larger strategy to be portrayed as serious about defense. "Clinton knew she could never advance her career—or win the presidency, especially—if she didn't prove that she was tough enough to be commander in chief," they write. "Female candidates, it's presumed, have often suffered as a result of the stereotype that they could never be as strong as men. Now the defense of the homeland had become such a paramount issue that Americans insisted their president—man or woman—protect them from another terrorist attack."[13] Moreover, the Republicans she had to face in 2008, such as Rudy Giuliani and Mitt Romney, organized their entire campaigns around the terrorist threat. Despite her tough stance, they hammered her consistently as weak on defense, subtly hinting that after 9/11 no woman was tough enough to meet the challenge.

Whatever the reason for Clinton's positions, she is a more hawkish candidate than Edwards or Obama, and has a record of supporting U.S. militarism. In 2004, the nonpartisan *National Journal*'s influential assessment rated her more conservative on foreign policy issues than forty-one other senators, making her among the most hawkish of Senate Democrats. Other evidence of Clinton's hegemonic politics, deeply at odds with a feminized foreign policy and worldview, includes: her 2003 Iraq vote; her 2002 vote against an amendment that would have required Bush to secure U.N. agreement before sending troops into Iraq; her service on a major Pentagon advisory committee that reinforced her reputation as the "Pentagon's favorite Democrat"; her repeated votes for authorization of spending on the Afghan and Iraqi wars; her 2006 vote against an amendment fixing a firm date for withdrawal of troops from Iraq; her 2007 vote supporting Bush's proposal to label the Iranian Revolutionary Guard as a terrorist organization; her long record of supporting a larger military; her hardline support for Israel—including refusal to denounce Ariel Sharon's long policy of promoting Jewish settlements in the West Bank, never speaking or voting against Israeli forces demolishing and walling off Palestinian villages in occupied territories, and supporting most recently Israel's 2006 war in Lebanon; her support of authoritarian regimes allied to the United States, including the dictatorships of Pakistan, Saudi Arabia, and Kuwait; and her long defense of repeated U.S. military interventions and regime changes such as the overthrow of Saddam Hussein.[14]

Clinton's support of the War on Terror seriously conflicts with feminized values. In a heated exchange between Edwards and Clinton during a 2007 New Hampshire debate over the Bush administration's fight against terrorism, reporters asked how the candidates saw Bush's war on terrorism. Edwards called it "a global war on terror bumper sticker—political slogan, that's all it is." But Clinton disagreed: "I'm a senator from New York. I have lived with the aftermath of 9/11. I believe we are safer than we were. We are not safe yet."[15]

Agreeing with the Bush administration's War on Terror rhetoric does not simply make Clinton "tough"; it aligns her with a militarized foreign policy, a masculinized fear campaign, and the masculinized protectionist model that accompanies it. Clinton's support for a militarized War on Terror has special implications for her authenticity as a feminized leader. The War on Terror has been sold to the public as in the best interest for women—protecting the women and children of the United States while rescuing the women of Afghanistan. Like a knight in shining armor, Bush promised to save the women of Afghanistan. He promised to fight "over there" to protect women and children at home. When Clinton supports the War on Terror, she betrays the feminized majority not only by endorsing a "long war" of endless violence but also by tacitly reinforcing the use of rhetoric defending women to sell a deeply masculinized foreign policy.

The gendered nature of post-9/11 politics became visible almost immediately. In October 2001, *Newsweek* columnist Jonathan Alter blasted progressives who suggest that America's militarism might explain the 9/11 attacks. He writes, "Talk about ironic: the same people always urging us to not blame the victim in rape cases are now saying Uncle Sam wore a skirt and asked for it."[16] Alter's sexual assault analogy implies that a country that is attacked is like a woman, and the attackers are like men. Equating critics of imperialism to women is no coincidence; feminized values in a time of war are very threatening to masculinized culture.

Although Clinton has come to oppose the Iraq War, her steadfast support of the War on Terror aids and abets the marketing of violence in the name of male honor and female vulnerability. The support for such patriarchal, military values in a hegemonic nation is incompatible with feminized morality. Clinton has not explicitly used language that degrades women or equates antiwar positions with female weakness, but her support of the War on Terror and U.S. hegemony seriously undermines feminized values.

Female politicians—especially progressives—face many hurdles. They must fight sexism and stereotypes as they fight for office. Nevertheless, the feminized majority rightly expects the feminized Clinton forcefully to oppose the Iraq War and broader U.S. militarism. Being strong under pressure does not mean being militaristic and hegemonic in foreign policy; from a feminized perspective, it means having the strength to assert feminized values in a masculinized foreign policy establishment. Militaristic Republican candidates such as Giuliani and Romney made this difficult for her, and it will take strong action by grassroots feminized groups to turn Clinton securely toward a less militarized model of strength.

Corporate Clinton

According to *Fortune* magazine, Hillary Clinton had some sharp words about corporate America at a recent campaign stop in Washington, D.C. "Let's start holding corporate America accountable, make them pay their fair share again," she said. "Enough with the corporate welfare! Enough with the golden parachutes! And enough with the tax incentives for companies to ship jobs overseas. We have to make sure there is not a single benefit they would get for doing that."[17] Cheers erupted from the audience.

Clinton's relationship with corporations is far more complex than her speech conveyed. Journalist Ari Berman shows a different side of the Clinton campaign in his article "Hillary, Inc." He writes, "Not only is Hillary more reliant on large donations and corporate money than her Democratic rivals, but advisers in her inner circle are closely affiliated with union busters, GOP operatives, conservative media, and other Democratic Party antagonists."[18] Berman illuminates the third profile of Clinton 2008: Corporate Hillary, a masculinized corporate ally. Corporate Clinton contradicts and constrains Village Clinton, presenting such a confusing picture that some voters view her as liberal or even socialist while others see her as a corporate toady.

Corporate Clinton fits the masculinized profile of earlier Democratic presidents in corporate regimes, from Grover Cleveland to Bill Clinton. Berman outlines the partnerships between the Hillary Clinton 2008 campaign and corporate lobbyists. Her campaign manager, Terry McAuliffe, is a longtime corporate insider and lobbyist with close ties to Wall Street and major Fortune 500 companies. Mark Penn, Hillary Clinton's pollster and chief strategist, is CEO of the PR firm Burson-Marsteller. The firm has collaborated with "everyone from the Argentine military junta to Union Carbide after the 1984 Bhopal disaster in India." It also "pioneered the use of pseudo-grassroots front groups ... to wage stealth corporate attacks against environmental and consumer groups."[19] Examples of such groups include the National Smokers

Alliance, which supported Philip Morris in the early 1990s; and the Clean and Safe Energy Coalition, which acts in the interests of the nuclear power industry. In 2006, the firm, not surprisingly, gave 57 percent of its political contributions to Republicans.[20]

Clinton has developed a close relationship with media mogul Rupert Murdoch, a reigning symbol of the hyper-masculinized corporate world. Murdoch, who owns Fox News and its parent company, Newscorp, is an aggressive corporate predator who seeks worldwide dominance over virtually all sectors of the mass media, entertainment, and news business. Murdoch and his son recently made gigantic contributions to the Clinton campaign. She also has the support of Morgan Stanley CEO John Mack—who previously secured over $200,000 for the Bush/Cheney campaign as a "Ranger."[21]

The most important of her corporate friends has been Robert Rubin, a leading Wall Street financier who advises her and, some speculate, could be her treasury secretary if she is elected. He was treasury secretary during her husband's presidency and steered the conservative fiscal policy that helped gut social programs and turn Bill Clinton—by his own admission—into the mold of an "Eisenhower Republican." With Hillary by his side and tutored by Rubin, Bill Clinton said the "era of big government is over," and he tried to make it happen. He worked hard to end welfare; closed down more than 130 government agencies, including those concerned with the environment, health, and education; privatized many government functions; and subsidized huge business enterprises, ranging from ag-business farm subsidies to timber and mining tax breaks and land giveaways. While Bill Clinton was ending welfare for the poor, he was lavishing billions of welfare dollars on America's biggest companies, about $300 billion annually according to the Cato Institute, a conservative Washington think tank.[22] In the 1990s, the Clintons were burying the New

Deal, the most important feminized policy revolution in twentieth-century America.

Given Hillary Clinton's own reliance on fundraising from big business and her close corporate ties as a senator, Clinton, unsurprisingly, votes frequently for corporate priorities. In 2004, Clinton supported the interests of the U.S. Chamber of Commerce 50 percent of the time, and in 2002, 45 percent of the time. In 2003–2004, she voted the preferred position of the American Road and Transportation Builders Association 88 percent of the time and the American Forest and Paper Association 41 percent of the time. In 2006, she voted 71 percent of the time to protect the interests of one of her favorite business groups, the National Stone, Sand, and Gravel Association. In 2001–2002, she gained a 58 percent record of support for the most important priorities of the Concord Coalition, a leading conservative force for budget austerity and a proponent of reducing or privatizing major feminized social spending programs such as Social Security and Medicare in the name of balanced budgets.[23]

Corporate America promotes advancing globalization through a probusiness trade agenda. Throughout the 1990s, both Clintons supported the probusiness, neoliberal trade principles of the World Trade Organization and the austere, privatization dictates for poor countries imposed by the International Monetary Fund and the World Bank. These institutions advocate masculinized policies by placing the main burden on workers and the poor, who are unprotected by trade agreements and social regulations, thus violating the feminized principles of equality and compassion. Bill Clinton sponsored NAFTA, one of big business's most cherished priorities, and Hillary Clinton supports "free trade" and corporate globalization, although, along with most other Democrats, she has softened her hardline neoliberalism and begun to respond to public pressure to support labor and environmental rights as part of a slightly more feminized trade regime.

Hillary Clinton is a complex politician. In 2007 campaign speeches, she often sounded more like the feminized Village Clinton, critical of unchecked corporate power. On a campaign stop in May, she remarked, "Unfortunately, for the past six years it's as though we've gone back to the era of the Robber Barons. Year after year the president has handed out massive tax breaks to oil companies, no-bid contracts to Halliburton, tax incentives to corporations shipping jobs overseas, tax cut after tax cut to multimillionaires, while ignoring the needs and aspirations of tens of millions of working families."[24]

But Corporate Clinton resists the strong action that would threaten the corporate regime and significantly limit corporate power. True, in the spirit of the Village, Clinton has supported many incremental corporate reforms. She has sought to repeal tax cuts for the rich, pass campaign finance reform, regulate the excesses associated with Enron and WorldCom, and keep funding alive for education, retraining, health, and child care. Most important, she has voted consistently to advance unions and support their agenda. In 2006, she voted in support of the Service Employees International Union 96 percent of the time; in 2005–2006, she supported the interests of the Brotherhood of Electrical Workers 75 percent of the time; in 2005 she supported the Boilermakers 100 percent of the time, the Service Workers 100 percent of the time, the United Auto Workers 93 percent of the time, and the AFL-CIO 93 percent of the time. This consistent support of labor led the National Journal to rate her economic performance in 2005 as more liberal than 84 percent of her fellow senators.[25] However, Clinton has yet to speak out on issues that would truly threaten corporate power, and lead America into a feminized, populist era. If she wants to transform the country and keep faith with her feminized base, she will need to embrace a more robust reform agenda restraining both corporate power and US militarism.

Despite some of our misgivings about Clinton's hegemonic and corporate tendencies, we are still hopeful
about prospects for a new American direction under a
Hillary Clinton administration. Having lived and worked
in the White House for eight years, President Hillary
Clinton would hit the ground running. Her experience
endows her with the toughness and credibility to change
course from the Bush years and to fight the inevitable
all-out blitz by hypermasculinized Republicans to undermine her and preserve their conservative hegemonic
regime. No other candidate, Democrat or Republican,
is better prepared to take over the Oval Office. Clinton
is working hard to convince skeptical liberals that, if
elected, she would truly act in their best interest to end
the Iraq War, shift from militarism to diplomacy, and
build a national Village for working families in America.
And her lead at this writing in 2007 suggests many of
these voters believe her.

Although Edwards and Obama have more explicitly
promised major reforms, many feminized voters are betting that Clinton can deliver at the ballot box and then actually achieve significant reforms that will move America
in the right direction. And Clinton may prove them correct.
Although her campaign rhetoric maintains the centrist
sensibilities of the Bill Clinton era, her progressive supporters swear she will provide the reforms the feminized
majority wants. For example, while she hasn't vehemently
demanded a pullout date for troops in Iraq, she has hinted
that, as president, she would support such a measure,
claiming that if this president (Bush) "doesn't end this
war, I will." Her health care plan retains many of the core
ideals of the Health Care Task Force she spearheaded in
1993; it is universal, mandatory, and has a significant
government component. And she has been more cautious
than Bill Clinton in accepting free trade agreements, voting against CAFTA. It might be that Hegemonic Clinton
and Corporate Clinton serve as the necessary armor

Village Clinton must wear in order to survive the battle of becoming the first woman president.

Boston Globe columnist Ellen Goodman believes Clinton's centrism is essential to overcoming the sexism plaguing women who run for political office. "The stakes and styles are still different for women," she writes. "The late Elizabeth Janeway once predicted that the first woman president would be a Republican. She'd defuse her sex by conservatism. Hillary is no Republican, nor is she Margaret Thatcher. But women walk a fine line to erase a gender line. So this is where Clinton is ... walking that line. While Obama gets praise for making history, she gets points for experience. ... When Edwards outflanks her on the left, this 'polarizing figure' settles deeper into the comforting center. It's the best place for a woman in the general election."[26]

Regardless of our serious qualms with some of Clinton's ideas and strategies, her presence in this race is electrifying for feminism and feminized politics, and will inspire future generations of women and feminized males to pursue public office. Clinton has given hope and confidence to women and girls everywhere. And it goes without saying that Clinton's corporate and hegemonic tendencies seem trivial when one imagines the damage any one of the hypermasculinized Republican candidates would inflict upon America and the world should the Democrats lose in November. The first, crucial step toward a more feminized America is Democrats taking back the White House, with Hillary in a strong position to do so. The future will then depend on the relationship between the new Democratic president and the grassroots feminized movements who seek to transform America. The feminized majority will support her candidacy because they recognize that any Republican will lock us in a hypermasculinized American regime, while a grassroots feminized tide can engage with Clinton and help her move the nation in a new, feminized direction.

CONCLUSION

The Victory Party

Democrats are tired of losing. They suffered eight years of conservative rule under Reagan, four under George H. W. Bush, and then eight *truly* agonizing years under George W. Bush. Many progressives felt a tremendous rush of relief when Democrats won both houses of Congress in 2006. At this writing, they smell victory in 2008 and are hungry for their party to occupy the White House. The new feminized majority can carry Democrats to victory in 2008 and beyond. It has the potential to create the ultimate makeover of the Democratic Party, from a losing party to a victory party.

To make this scenario work, two things must happen. First, the Democrats must change their political strategy to engage and mobilize the new feminized majority. Second, they need to sustain a new intimate dance with grassroots social movements that carry feminized values and have the passion to change the country over the long term. The Democrats' long-term ascendancy as a victory party will be the result of an enduring, winning connection between the Democratic Party and an activist feminized majority.

Sustaining Victory

American GIs found it easy to take Baghdad but hard to occupy it and change Iraq. Democrats may face a similar situation. The debacle of Republican rule and deep anger at Bush may propel the Democrats into the White House no matter what strategy they use. But while one can pleasantly imagine a 2009 scenario of Democrats controlling both the White House and Congress, the consequences of the occupation are not necessarily what the feminized majority wants. Feminized majoritarians want and need a regime change: from the third corporate regime to a new regime based on their own universalistic values. Even after a 2008 victory, the Democratic Party will remain a member in good standing of the corporate regime, as it was during the years of Bill Clinton.

If we envision Hillary Clinton in the White House in 2009, the Village Clinton will be contending with Hegemonic Clinton and Corporate Clinton. Which Clinton will get the upper hand? The war *within* Hillary will be won by the war *outside* her. Military hawks, big corporations, and the New Democrats will aid and abet Hegemonic and Corporate Clinton. But the feminized majority—all the grassroots movements and feminized voters who propelled her into office—will push and promote Village Clinton. The direction taken by Clinton and the Democratic Party will be determined by a larger struggle between feminized populists and the third corporate regime.

This regime-change fight will shape the future of the Democratic Party, but history suggests that a Democratic victory in 2008 could be the best way to move the regime-change struggle forward, whichever Hillary Clinton emerges on top. And the same would be true if it is a President Obama or Edwards, each of whom has their own dueling Village and Hegemonic/Corporate sides. This is because the relative balance of power between the regime and the feminized majority tends to shift when a Democrat is in power. Even a Hegemonic or Corporate Clinton will open up possibilities for the feminized majority, and the feminized base will help tip the balance of power from Corporate/Hegemonic to Village Clinton.[1]

Two historical scenarios point to this outcome. When Franklin Roosevelt became president in 1932, he inherited a masculinized, laissez-faire corporate morality from Herbert Hoover and the second corporate regime of the 1920s. His first instincts were to cope with the Depression with Hooverist corporate self-regulation supported by big business. But his election electrified the Democratic grass roots that had heard a whiff of his populist inclinations in the campaign. His election helped catalyze wildcat strikes by industrial workers and urban riots by evicted tenants. All the populists needed was a shred of hope—and FDR's election cracked open a window just wide enough to mobilize the growing labor and social justice movements.

The activism on the ground, in turn, had a catalyzing impact on FDR. His progressive side bloomed and his corporate side receded along with the second corporate regime. With the rousing populist endorsement of his landslide reelection in 1936, FDR cut his ties with the corporate regime and laid the foundation of the New Deal, the most important regime change in modern U.S. history.[2] Roosevelt undertook a new politics of values, collaborating with the populist movements to challenge and discredit the hard-edged corporate morality of the 1920s and of the 1890s Gilded Age era. The dance between Roosevelt and the populist grassroots movements changed the country. It also turned the New Deal Democratic Party into a values-driven victory party, based on more universalistic, egalitarian, and feminized progressive principles. It enjoyed ascendancy for almost half a century.[3]

A second historical example of the catalyzing relationship between Democrats and social movements is the election of John F. Kennedy in 1960. Kennedy was a cold warrior and corporate ally, although he had a progressive streak. Like Hillary Clinton, he was a centrist Democrat of his time, and he ran and was elected on a dual image of masculinized toughness and feminized liberal sympathies.

The masculinized JFK was dominant as Kennedy moved into the White House. Nonetheless, his election opened up space for a whole new generation of populist and feminized social movements, which had remained dormant during the 1950s Eisenhower Republican era. Young people tuned into Kennedy's liberal idealism rather than his hegemonic or corporate sides, sensing a new age of possibilities that Kennedy symbolized. The result was the most dramatic moral revolution in modern America. The civil rights movement, the student peace and justice movements, new environmental movements, and the rise of women and feminist movements all brought a hurricane of new moral passions into the public square.[4] A new feminized populism was taking form.

The early stirrings of these values-driven movements—led by Martin Luther King and the Southern sit-ins against segregated lunch counters—helped catalyze Lyndon Johnson's Great Society program in 1964. Empowered by the movements, liberal Democrats, led by LBJ, felt freer to assert their more feminized, populist values and transform them into legislation. This legislative action, in turn, opened up more space for the movements, which became more radical and imaginative, pushing the envelope of cultural and moral transformation.

The Vietnam War aborted this cycle of the dance between the Democratic Party and social movements. Johnson and the Democratic Party embraced the Mars of war, and became the enemy of the just-emerging Venus, the party's rising feminized base. The movements now sought to sustain a revolutionary politics of values on their own, while the Democrats abandoned the Great Society vision and slowly lost their New Deal moral compass.[5]

This disconnect between the Democratic Party and the new feminized base proved tragic. It opened up space for the New Right and a resurgent masculinized moral backlash that carried Ronald Reagan to power. The feminized, populist values of the 1960s movements were portrayed by the Republicans as subversive of all morality.[6] The Democrats capitulated to this moral backlash, abandoning the values of the New Deal and giving Republicans control of the moral debate in Washington. Traditional values became the core of "values" politics, since Democrats offered no clear alternative.[7]

Nonetheless, feminized values survived and continued to grow among the populace.[8] While Nixon and Reagan spoke to what they called the silenced "Moral Majority," the feminized majority was the true silenced majority. Since they had no political party that spoke for their values, they tried to live their own lives and shape their local communities in the spirit of feminized values. But Republicans ran the national government on very different values. The feminized majority—demoralized by the victorious masculinized backlash—receded as a visible national political force.

The same demoralization crippled the Democratic Party. It became a loser party after 1980, lacking in values and vision. Its moral connection with the feminized majority was broken. Feminized voters no longer saw the party as a political home, and the party drifted toward the yellow line in the center of the highway, having no moral compass to guide it. Without the feminized base, the party had no backbone, energy, or values.

George W. Bush and an extremist Republican Party has now offered the opportunity of a generation for the Democrats and feminized majority to reconnect. Bush's Martian policies of class warfare inside America and hegemonic warfare against the world have brought the Democratic Party and the feminized majority together in a common passion to end Republican rule. The intensely masculinized Republican backlash has finally produced its own backlash among feminized voters. It has also stirred populist sentiments among Democratic politicians, who sense the intensity of feeling in the Democratic base.

Will a Democratic victory in 2008 catalyze again the magical synergy between the Democratic Party and grassroots movements that created regime-change politics under FDR in the 1930s and a moral revolution in the 1960s? It is a real possibility.[9] The harshness of hypermasculinized capitalism has taken a heavy toll on ordinary Americans, and the failed wars in the Middle East have put in question the machismo militarism of U.S. foreign policy. Structural conditions are making America ripe for a feminized regime change.

The American public is responding as one might expect to these adverse circumstances. According to polling data, the spread of feminized values in the populace is accelerating,[10] even touching many evangelical youth who feel betrayed by the moral corruption of the Republicans and the lies of the Bush administration. America is not in a depression but a strong populist mood is rippling across the country. And, as in the 1960s, the catastrophe of a bloody, failed war has called into question the most important masculinized value—war and aggression—opening a new window for a feminized vision of patriotism and foreign policy.

Moreover, technology is facilitating new connecting threads that are already producing synergy between the movements and the Democratic Party.[11] We saw this phenomenon in Howard Dean's campaign, and see it again in groups like MoveOn.org that have pioneered the use of the Internet to send populist messages with teeth to the Democrats, while helping to build the collective consciousness of the base with meetups and house parties. A whole new generation of feminized bloggers, comedians, and web-savvy young people are using the weapons of YouTube and Myspace to transform American politics. Suddenly, ordinary Americans who have never voted or connected with the political process are jumping in to virtual politics with a passion.

This has special significance for the Democrats, because they have not had the institutionalized spaces like megachurches to connect with the feminized majority, and cannot rely on megacorporate funding like the Republicans. *The Democrats' best hope, in 2008 and beyond, is to catch the wave of populist energy emanating from the feminized majority.* If Democratic politicians get the message and frame an agenda driven by the feminized majority's values, people will become more energized and put yet more feminized, populist pressure on the party.

The biggest contradiction in American politics today is the "values gap" between the political establishment in Washington and the feminized majority. The Democrats can become a governing party for the next generation if they align themselves with the values of this new majority. The feminized majority wants the country to change. The Democrats can turn themselves into an enduring victory party if they embrace the feminized values of the American people. If they create a feminized twenty-first-century New Deal based on the majoritarian values of the nation, they will help America live up to its democratic ideals. This populist vision seems common sense, but it is a lot to ask of a corporate party in a corporate regime. Nonetheless, it offers a path to Democratic Party ascendancy in the coming generation. All it takes is a new democratic will by the Democratic Party to connect to the majority and respond to their deepest moral aspirations. Democrats must speak to the needs and values of the true moral majority.

NOTES

Notes to Introduction

1. Associated Press, "Election Reinforces USA's Religious Schism," *USA Today,* 8 November 2004.
2. Ibid.
3. Charisse Jones, "Issues: 11 States Nix Gay Marriage; California OKs Stem-Cell Work," *USA Today,* 5 November 2004.
4. George G. Hunter, III, *Christian, Evangelical, and . . . Democrat?* (Nashville, TN: Abingdon, 2006).
5. Dana Milbank, "For President, a Vote of Full Faith and Credit," *Washington Post,* 7 November 2004, A7.
6. CNN Exit Poll, www.cnn.com/ELECTION/2004/pages/results/states/US/P/00/epolls.0.html. Accessed 20 October 2007.
7. David Gauthier, "Thomas Hobbes: Moral Theorist," *Journal of Philosophy* 76 (1979): 547–559.

Notes to Chapter One

1. John Gray, *Men Are from Mars, Women Are from Venus* (New York: Quill, 1992), 2.
2. Ibid., 9.
3. Ibid., 11.
4. Simone de Beauvoir, *The Second Sex* (New York: Knopf, 1989), 65.
5. Francine M. Deutsch, "Undoing Gender," *Gender and Society* 21 (2007): 106.
6. CNN Exit Poll, http://www.cnn.com/ELECTION/2004/pages/results/states/US/P/00/epolls.0.html. Accessed 20 October 2007.
7. George Lakoff, *Moral Politics* (Chicago: University of Chicago Press, 1996), 73.
8. Ibid., 110–113.

Notes to Chapter Two

1. Within the vast literature on the Puritans, three particularly helpful sources are Edmund S. Morgan, *The Puritan Dilemma: The Story of John Winthrop* (New York: Longman, 2006); David D. Hall, ed., *Puritans in the New World: A Critical Anthology* (Princeton, NJ: Princeton University Press, 2004); and David D. Hall, *Worlds of Wonder, Days of Judgment* (Cambridge, MA: Harvard University Press, 1990).

2. Hall, *Worlds of Wonder, Days of Judgment.*

3. Morgan, *The Puritan Dilemma.*

4. Ibid. The quote from George Washington is cited in William A. Williams, *Empire as a Way of Life* (New York: Oxford University Press, 1990), 43.

5. Cyclone Covey, *The Gentle Radical* (New York: Macmillan, 1966); and Edmund S. Morgan, *Roger Williams: The Church and the State* (New York: Harcourt, Brace, 1967).

6. Hall, *Puritans in the New World.*

7. Max Weber, *The Protestant Ethic and the Spirit of Capitalism,* 2nd rev. ed. (New York: HarperCollins, 1997).

8. Alan Dershowitz, *Rights from Wrongs* (New York: Basic Books, 2004).

9. Williams, *Empire as a Way of Life.*

10. Edward Levy, *American Constitutional Law: Historical Essays* (New York: Harper Torchbooks, 1966).

11. Charles A. Beard, *An Economic Interpretation of the Constitution of the United States* (New York: Dover, 2004).

12. Robert Dahl, *How Democratic Is the American Constitution?* 2nd ed. (New Haven, CT: Yale University Press, 2003).

13. Williams, *Empire as a Way of Life,* 45.

14. Thomas Jefferson, *On Politics and Government* (Charlottesville: University of Virginia Press, 1809). For a commentary on Jefferson's reflections on empire and the Louisiana Purchase, see Williams, *Empire as a Way of Life,* 59ff.

15. Frederick Jackson Turner, *The Frontier in American History* (New York: Dover, 2007).

16. Without using the gendered terms, Jeremy Rifkin makes a similar argument to differentiate the United States and Europe. See Jeremy Rifkin, *The European Dream* (New York: Tarcher/Penguin Books, 2004).

17. Charles Derber with Yale Magrass, *Morality Wars: How Americans Do Evil in the Name of Good* (Boulder, CO: Paradigm Publishers, 2008).

18. The discussion of the Gilded Age here relies on Charles Derber, *Corporation Nation* (New York: St. Martin's, 2000), Chapter 1.

19. Cited in ibid., 22.

20. Ibid.

21. For further discussion of this masculinized frontier moral code, see Derber and Magrass, *Morality Wars.* Chapter 2.

22. Morgan, *The Puritan Dilemma.*

23. See Christopher Hill, *The Century of Revolution, 1603–1714* (New York: Norton, 1961).

24. Williams, *Empire as a Way of Life,* 43.

25. Ibid.

26. Cited in ibid., 55.

27. Theodore Roosevelt, *The Rough Riders* (New York: Charles Scribner's Sons, 1899; reprint New York: Dover, 2006); Woodrow Wilson, "Address to the United States Senate on Essential Terms of Peace in Europe," 22 January 1917.

28. Andrew Jackson, "Address to Congress," 3 December 1833, cited in Derber and Magrass, *Morality Wars,* 42.

29. Ibid.

30. John L. Sullivan, "The Great Nation of Futurity," *United States Democratic Review* 6, no. 23 (1839): 426–430.

31. Stephen Austin, "Speech in Louisville, Kentucky, March 7, 1836," cited in Derber and Magrass, *Morality Wars,* 44.

32. Ibid.

33. Cited in James MacGregor, *The Three Roosevelts: Patrician Leaders Who Transformed America* (Berkeley, CA: Grove Press, 2001), 45.

34. Ibid.

Notes to Chapter Three

1. Pippa Norris, "The Gender Gap: Old Challenges, New Approaches," http://ksghome.harvard.edu/~pnorris/acrobat/rutgers.pdf. Accessed 20 October 2007.

2. See Karen DeYoung, "Spy Agencies Say Iraq War Hurting U.S. Terror Fight," *Washington Post,* 24 September 2006, A01.

3. *Public Papers of the Presidents of the United States: Lyndon B. Johnson, 1963–1964*, vol. 1, 112–118 (Washington, DC: Government Printing Office, 1965), http://www.lbjlib.utexas.edu/johnson/archives.hom/speeches.hom/640108.asp. Accessed 20 July 2007.

4. Ibid.

5. Peter Grier and Patrik Jonsson, "In War on Poverty, Early Gains and a Long Stalemate," *Christian Science Monitor,* 9 January 2004, http://www.csmonitor.com/2004/0109/p01s02-ussc.html. Accessed 18 November 2007.

6. Commission on Presidential Debates, www.debates.org/pages/ trans96a.html. Accessed 20 October 2007.

7. Roger Lowenstein, "The Inequality Conundrum," *New York Times Magazine*, 10 June 2007, http://select.nytimes.com/ preview/2007/06/10/magazine/1154677963736.html. Accessed 18 November 2007.

8. Matt Bai, "The Poverty Platform," *New York Times Magazine*, 10 June 2007, http://www.nytimes.com/2007/06/10/magazine/ 10edwards-t.html. Accessed 18 November 2007.

9. "America's Richest," *Forbes Magazine*, 21 September 2006, http://www.forbes.com/lists/2006/54/biz_06rich400_The-400-Richest-Americans_land.html. Accessed 20 October 2007.

10. See Andrew Bacevich, *American Empire: The Realities and Consequences of U.S. Diplomacy* (Cambridge, MA: Harvard University Press, 2002).

11. Robert Kagan, *Of Paradise and Power: America and Europe in the New World Order* (New York: Vintage, 2003), 4.

12. Ibid., 5.

13. Ibid., 3 (emphasis added).

14. Ibid., 6.

15. Ibid., 32.

16. Ibid., 27.

17. The definitive source of data on the national distribution of global production shares is the World Bank. See the World Development Report, published by the World Bank each year over the last twenty-eight years. For commentary and data on the U.S. share of global production after World War II, see Paul Kennedy, *The Rise and Fall of the Great Powers* (New York: Random House, 1987), 358ff.

18. See Immanual Wallerstein, *The Decline of American Power* (New York: Norton, 2003).

19. See World Bank, *World Development Report 2007* (New York: United Nations, 2007). For an account of changes in the distribution of national shares of global economic production over time, see *World Development Report 1978–2006 with Multiple Indicators 2005*, indexed omnibus CD-rom, 2005 (New York: United Nations, 2006).

20. See Charles Derber, *People before Profit* (New York: Picador, 2003). See also Charles Derber, *Hidden Power* (San Francisco: Berrett-Koehler, 2005).

21. For an excellent account of the role of military spending in shifting economic hegemony from the United States to East Asia, see Giovanni Arrighi, *Adam Smith in Beijing* (London: Verso, 2007).

22. Ibid. See also Giovanni Arrighi and Beverly Silver, *Chaos and Governance in the Modern World System* (Minneapolis: University of Minnesota Press, 1999).

23. See Charles Derber with Yale Magrass, *Morality Wars* (Boulder, CO: Paradigm Publishers, 2008).

24. See the polling data discussed in Chapter 4 of this book, particularly Gallup and Pew polls that show the weakening of popular commitment to American global dominance.

25. Karen Kaufmann, "Culture Wars, Secular Realignment, and the Gender Gap," *Political Behavior* 24 (2002): 288.

26. See Derber with Magrass, *Morality Wars*, for a full discussion of this moral backlash.

27. See the polling data documented in detail in the next chapter.

Notes to Chapter Four

1. Harris poll conducted 5 February 2007, http://www.harrisinteractive.com/harris_poll/index.asp?PID=725. Accessed 18 November 2007.

2. CNN exit poll, www.cnn.com/ELECTION/2004/pages/results. Accessed 16 October 2007.

3. CNN exit poll, www.cnn.com/ELECTION/2000/results/index.epolls.html. Accessed 16 October 2007.

4. Karen Kaufmann, "Culture Wars, Secular Realignment, and the Gender Gap," *Political Behavior* 24 (2002): 283.

5. Janet Elder, "Soccer Moms Are So 1996. Try Wal-Mart Women," *New York Times, Week in Review,* 23 September 2007, 14.

6. *New York Times/CBS News* poll conducted September 2007, cited in ibid.

7. *New York Times/CBS News* poll conducted July 2007, cited in ibid.

8. *New York Times/ CBS News* poll conducted 20 December 2003, www.cbsnews.com/stories/2003/12/19/opinion/polls/main589551.shtml. Accessed 18 November 2007.

9. "Abortion and Rights of Terror Suspects Top Court Issues," Pew Research Center, 3 August 2005, http://www.people-press.org/reports/display.php3?ReportID=253. Accessed 18 November 2007.

10. "Hard Times for Bush and the GOP," *Los Angeles Times/* Bloomberg poll conducted 12 April 2006, http://www.latimes.com/media/acrobat/2006-04/22915725.pdf. Accessed 18 November 2007.

11. Celinda Lake and Kellyanne Conway, *What Women Really Want* (New York: Free Press, 2005), 211.

12. "Many Americans Uneasy with Mix of Religion and Politics," Pew poll conducted 24 August 2006, http://www.pewforum.org/docs/index.php?DocID=153. Accessed 18 November 2007.

13. Kaufmann, "Culture Wars," 283.

14. Susan Howell and Christine Day, "Complexities of the Gender Gap," *Journal of Politics* 62 (2000): 858.

15. Ibid.

16. Anna Greenberg, "Do Real Men Vote Democratic?" *American Prospect*, 23 October 2000.

17. *CBS News* poll conducted 12 September 2001, http://www.ropercenter.uconn.edu.ezproxy.library.drexel.edu/ipoll.html. Accessed 18 November 2007.

18. Kathleen A. Frankovic, "Sex and Politics—New Alignments, Old Issues," *PS: Political Science and Politics* 15 (1982): 439–448.

19. *ABC News/Washington Post* poll conducted 20–23 May 2004, http://www.abcnews.go.com/sections/us/Polls/torture_poll_040527.html. Accessed 18 November 2007.

20. Pew poll, http://www.people-press.org/reports/display.php3?ReportID=273. Accessed 16 October 2007.

21. CNN/*Time* exit poll, http://www.cnn.com/ALLPOLITICS/1996/elections/natl.exit.poll/index1.html. Accessed 16 October 2007.

22. Pew Research Center, "Trends in Political Values and Core Attitudes: 1987–2007," 22 March 2007, 1, http://www.people-press.org/reports/pdf/312.pdf. Accessed 15 October 2007.

23. Campaign for America's Future, "The Progressive Majority: Why a Conservative America Is a Myth," June 2007, http://home.ourfuture.org/assets/20070612_theprogressivemajority_report.pdf. Accessed 15 October 2007.

24. Pew Research Center, "Trends in Political Values and Core Attitudes: 1987–2007," 1.

25. 2004 National Election Studies Survey cited in Campaign for America's Future, "The Progressive Majority: Why a Conservative America Is a Myth," 3.

26. Ibid.

27. Robin Toner and Janet Elder, "Most Support U.S. Guarantee of Health Care," *New York Times*, 2 March 2007, http://www.nytimes.com/2007/03/02/washington/02poll.html. Accessed 18 November 2007.

28. CNN/Opinion Research Corporation poll conducted 4–6 May 2007, http://i.a.cnn.net/cnn/2007/images/05/09/rel6e.pdf. Accessed 16 October 2007.

29. Gallup poll conducted 9–12 November 2006, http://www.galluppoll.com/content/Default.aspx?ci=4708&VERSION=p. Accessed 16 October 2007.

30. Associated Press/AOL News poll conducted by Ipsos Public Affairs, 19–21 December 2006, http://www.pollingreport.com/work. htm. Accessed 16 October 2007.

31. *Los Angeles Times*/Bloomberg poll conducted 12 December 2006, cited in Campaign for America's Future, "The Progressive Majority," 9.

32. CNN poll conducted by Opinion Research Corp., August 2006, http://edition.cnn.com/2006/POLITICS/09/07/poll/index.html. Accessed 16 October 2007.

33. Gallup poll conducted April 2007, cited in Campaign for America's Future, "The Progressive Majority," 9.

34. *NBC News* poll conducted 3–5 April 2005, http://www.msnbc. msn.com/id/7433834. Accessed 18 November 2007.

35. *NBC News/Wall Street Journal* poll conducted October 2005, cited in Campaign for America's Future, "The Progressive Majority," 9.

36. Pew Research Center for the People and the Press: Beyond Red versus Blue, the 2005 Political Typology, "Would You Say Your Overall Opinion of Labor Unions Is . . . ," 2007, http://typology.people-press. org/data/index.php?QuestionID=46. Accessed 15 October 2007.

37. Gallup poll conducted 8–11 August 2006, "Labor Unions: Do You Approve or Disapprove of Labor Unions?" http://www.galluppoll. com/content/default.aspx?ci=12751. Accessed 16 October 2007.

38. Ibid.

39. Gallup poll conducted 1977, cited in Campaign for America's Future, "The Progressive Majority," 12.

40. Gallup poll conducted 2006, cited in Campaign for America's Future, "The Progressive Majority," 12.

41. Pew poll conducted 22 March 2007, cited in Campaign for America's Future, "The Progressive Majority," 13.

42. Gallup poll conducted 2006, cited in Campaign for America's Future, "The Progressive Majority," 12.

43. Pew Research Center, "Trends in Political Values and Core Attitudes: 1987–2007," 37.

44. CNN/Opinion Research poll conducted May 2007, http://www. cnn.com/2007/US/06/27/poll.gay/index.html. Accessed 15 October 2007.

45. Gallup poll conducted 28–30 June 1982, http://www. galluppoll.com/content/?ci=27694&pg=1. Accessed 18 November 2007.

46. Pew Research Center, "Trends in Political Values and Core Attitudes: 1987–2007."

47. Ibid.

48. National Elections Studies, 1972–2004, "Views on the Role of Women," http://home.ourfuture.org/assets/20070612_theprogressivemajority_report.pdf. Accessed 18 November 2007.

49. Ibid.

50. *ABC News/Washington Post* poll conducted 18–21 July 2007, http://media.washingtonpost.com/wp-srv/politics/ssi/polls/post-poll_072307.html. Accessed 15 October 2007.

51. Quinnipiac University poll conducted August 2007, http://www.quinnipiac.edu/x1284.xml?ReleaseID=1093&What=&strArea=;&strTime=0. Accessed 15 October 2007.

52. Gallup poll conducted May 2007, http://www.galluppoll.com/content/?ci=27628. Accessed 15 October 2007.

53. *New York Times/CBS News* poll conducted 7 March 2007, http://thecaucus.blogs.nytimes.com/2007/04/10/public opinion on-abortion. Accessed 15 October 2007.

54. Pew Research Center, *The 2004 Political Landscape: Evenly Divided and Increasingly Polarized,* 5 November 2003, http://people-press.org/reports/pdf/196.pdf,, p. 47. Accessed 18 November 2007.

55. Pew poll conducted 14 May 2003, http://people-press.org/reports/display.php3?ReportID=184. Accessed 15 October 2007.

56. Zogby poll conducted in 2004, cited in Campaign for America's Future, "The Progressive Majority," 10.

57. Public Agenda and *Foreign Affairs,* cited in Campaign for America's Future. "The Progressive Majority," 14.

58. Ibid.

59. Pew Research Center. "Beyond Red versus Blue." 10 May 2005, 20, http://www.people-press.org/reports/pdf/242.pdf. Accessed 18 November 2007.

60. Pew Research Center, "Trends in Political Values and Core Attitudes: 1987–2007," 20.

61. Gallup poll conducted 1–4 February 2007, http://www.gallup.com/poll/26707/Americans-Pessimistic-About-US-Role-World.aspx#2. Accessed 15 October 2007.

62. *CBS News/New York Times* poll, 9 September 2007, http://www.cbsnews.com/stories/2007/09/09/opinion/polls/main3244734.shtml. Accessed 15 October 2007.

63. *New York Times/CBS News* poll conducted 18 July 2007, http://www.cbsnews.com/stories/2007/07/18/opinion/polls/main3071073.shtml. Accessed 16 October 2007; *USA Today*/Gallup poll cited in Reuters, "Most Americans Back Iraq Pullout Timetable," 9 May 2007. http://www.reuters.com/article/domesticNews/idUSN0921489720070509. Accessed 16 October 2007; *Washington Post/ABC News* poll cited in Dan Balz and Jon Cohen, "Majority in

Poll Favor Deadline for Iraq Pullout," *Washington Post*, 27 February 2007, p. A1.

64. CNN/Opinion Research Corporation poll conducted 21–23 April 2006, cited in *CNN News*, "Poll Suggests Iraq PR Push Falls Short," http://edition.cnn.com/2006/US/04/25/poll.war/index.html. Accessed 15 October 2007.

65. Pew poll conducted 17 November 2005, http://people-press. org/reports/display.php3?PageID=1020. Accessed 16 October 2007.

Notes to Chapter Five

1. Quoted in Michele Barrett, *Women's Oppression Today: The Marxist/Feminist Encounter* (London: Verso, 1980), 11.

2. Heidi Hartmann, "The Unhappy Marriage of Marxism and Feminism: Towards a More Progressive Union." Pp. 1–42 in Lydia Sargent, ed., *Women and Revolution: A Discussion of the Unhappy Marriage of Marxism and Feminism* (Boston: South End, 1981), 28.

3. British Labour Party website, http://www.labour.org.uk/ labour_policies. Accessed 16 October 2007.

4. See E. P. Thompson, *The Making of the English Working Class* (Gloucester: Peter Smith, 1999).

5. Charles Derber, *Corporation Nation* (New York: St. Martin's, 2000).

6. For a classic treatment of this subject, see Stanley Aronowitz, *False Promises* (Durham, NC: Duke University Press, 1992).

7. Audre Lorde, "The Master's Tools Will Never Dismantle the Master's House." Pp. 110–113 in Audre Lorde, *Sister Outsider: Essays and Speeches* (Trumansburg, NY: Crossing Press, 1984), 111.

8. CNN.com election results, http://www.cnn.com/ ELECTION/2004/pages/results/states/US/P/00/epolls.0.html. Accessed 16 October 2007.

9. See bell hooks, *Ain't I A Woman: Black Women and Feminism* (Boston: South End Press, 1981); and Patricia Hill Collins, *Black Feminist Thought: Knowledge, Consciousness, and the Politics of Empowerment* (New York: Routledge, 1990).

10. Jennifer Friedlin, "Second- and Third-Wave Feminists Clash Over the Future," *Women's e-News*, 26 May 2002, http://www. womensenews.org/article.cfm/dyn/aid/920/context/cover. Accessed 16 October 2007.

11. Ibid.

12. Ibid.

13. For a discussion of the more feminized European culture, see Jeremy Rifkin, *The European Dream* (New York: Tarcher/Penguin, 2004).

14. Derber, *Corporation Nation.*

15. AFL-CIO Constitution, http://www.aflcio.org/aboutus/thisistheaflcio/constitution/art00.cfm. Accessed 17 October 2007.

16. Pew Research Center for the People and the Press, "Republicans Divided about Role of Government: Democrats by Social and Personal Values," 10 May 2005, http://www.people-press.org/reports/display.php3?PageID=949. Accessed 17 October 2007.

Notes to Chapter Six

1. CNN exit poll, www.cnn.com/ELECTION/2004/pages/results/states/US/P/00/epolls.0.html. Accessed 17 October 2007.

2. Ibid.

3. Ibid.

4. Institute for Women's Policy Research, "Smaller Gender Gap in Crucial States May Have Cost Kerry the Election," 11 November 2004, http://www.iwpr.org/pdf/IWPR-Release-11-11-04.pdf. Accessed 17 October 2007.

5. "Gender Gap Myths and Legends." *Washington Times*, 19 December 2004, http://www.washingtontimes.com/op-ed/20041218-100132-6503r.htm.

6. "The Gender Gap in Politics Goes Deeper Than a Liberal-Conservative Split," *Stanford University News Service*, 30 October 1996, www.stanford.edu/dept/news/pr/96/961030gendergap.html. Accessed 17 October 2007.

7. Susan Howell and Christine Day, "Complexities of the Gender Gap," *Journal of Politics* 62 (2000): 858.

8. "Post-ABC Poll: Bush's Popularity Remains Strong," *Washington Post*, 17 July 2002, www.washingtonpost.com/wp-srv/politics/polls/vault/stories/data071602.htm; and Harris Interactive poll conducted 9–16 August 2005, http://www.ropercenter.uconn.edu.ezproxy.library.drexel.edu/ipoll/html. Accessed 18 November 2007.

9. Thomas Frank, *What's the Matter with Kansas?* (New York: Metropolitan, 2004).

10. See Charles Derber with Yale Magrass, *Morality Wars* (Boulder, CO: Paradigm Publishers, 2008).

11. See Matt Bai, *The Argument: Billionaires, Bloggers, and the Battle to Remake Democratic Politics* (New York: Penguin, 2007). See also Charles Derber, *Hidden Power* (San Francisco: Berrett-Koehler, 2005).

Notes to Chapter Seven

1. Ralph Nader, *Crashing the Party: Taking on the Corporate Government in an Age of Surrender* (New York: St. Martin's, 2002), 21.

2. Charles Derber, *Corporation Nation: How Corporations Are Taking Over Our Lives and What We Can Do about It* (New York: St. Martin's, 1998), 15.

3. For a detailed discussion of corporate regimes, see Charles Derber, *Hidden Power* (San Francisco: Berrett-Koehler, 2005). See also Derber, *Regime Change Begins at Home* (San Francisco: Berrett-Koehler, 2004).

4. Ibid.

5. Ibid., Chapter 1.

6. Cleveland, cited in Derber, *Corporation Nation*, 23.

7. Ibid.

8. For an excellent discussion of progressivism, see Gabriel Kolko, *The Triumph of Conservatism*. See also Derber, *Hidden Power*, for a discussion of the progressive regime.

9. Derber, *Hidden Power*, 32ff.

10. Ibid., 36.

11. For a discussion of the New Deal as a regime change from the 1920s, see Derber, *Hidden Power*.

12. For a detailed discussion, see Derber, *Hidden Power*, Chapter 2.

13. Ibid.

14. Derber, *Corporation Nation*.

15. Daniel Hellinger and Dennis R. Judd, *The Democratic Façade* (Pacific Grove, CA: Brooks/Cole, 1991), 147.

16. Ibid., 24.

17. Derber, *Corporation Nation*, 14.

18. Russell Feingold, "Turn Back Corporate Democracy," *Los Angeles Times*, 15 August 2000.

19. Robert Dreyfuss, "How the DLC Does It," *American Prospect*, 23 April 2001, http://www.prospect.org/cs/articles?article=how_the_dlc_does_it. Accessed 18 November 2007.

20. Thomas Frank, *What's the Matter with Kansas?* (New York: Metropolitan Books, 2004), 243.

21. John Nichols, "Behind the DLC Takeover," *Progressive*, October 2000, http://archives.indymedia.org/imc-editorial/2000-October/00604.html. Accessed 18 November 2007.

22. New Democratic Network, http://www.ndn.org.

23. Dreyfuss, "How the DLC Does It," *American Prospect*, 23 April 2001, http://www.prospect.org/cs/articles?article=how_the_dlc_does_it, Accessed 18 November 2007.

24. Ibid.

25. Ibid.

26. Howard Dean, *You Have the Power: How to Take Back Our Country and Restore Democracy in America* (New York: Simon and Schuster, 2006).

27. Ibid.

28. Edward Wasserman, "'Dean Scream' Clip Was Media Fraud," *Miami Herald*, 23 February 2005.

29. Joe Trippi, *The Revolution Will Not Be Televised* (New York: HarperCollins, 2004), 203.

30. Ibid.

31. Anna Greenberg, "Moving beyond the Gender Gap," Greenberg, Quinlan, Rosner Research. http://www.gqrr.com/index.php?ID=1663. Accessed 18 October 2007.

32. Alan Cooperman, "Democrats Win Bigger Share of Religious Vote," *Washington Post*, 11 November 2006, A1.

Notes to Chapter Eight

1. Ryan Lizza, "The Invasion of the Alpha-Male Democrat," *New York Times*, 7 January 2007, section 4, 1.

2. Ibid.

3. CNN exit poll, www.cnn.com/ELECTION/2006/pages/results/states/VA/S/01/index.html. Accessed 20 October 2007.

4. Lizza, "The Invasion of the Alpha-Male Democrat."

5. John Tester, "On the Issues," www.testerforsenate.com/issues. Accessed 20 October 2007.

6. CNN exit poll.

7. Anna Greenberg, "Do Real Men Vote Democratic?" *American Prospect*, 23 October 2000.

8. Ibid.

9. Tester, "On the Issues."

10. John Tester, "Time to Turn Our Attention to Regular Folks' Needs," *Billings Gazette*, 15 July 2006.

11. "Strong at Home, Respected in the World," *The 2004 Democratic National Platform for America* (2004), 12, http://www.democrats.org/pdfs/2004platform.pdf. Accessed 18 November 2007.

12. For elaboration of this analysis and of Democratic complicity in America's long embrace of imperial "immoral morality," see Charles Derber with Yale Magrass, *Morality Wars* (Boulder, CO: Paradigm Publishers, 2008).

13. This is all documented in extensive polling. See the 2005 Pew poll on religion and politics, http://pewforum.org/publications/surveys/religion-politics-05.pdf.

14. Harris poll conducted 7–10 July 2006, http://www.ropercenter/uconn.edu.ezproxy.library.drexel.edu/ipoll.html. Accessed 18 November 2007.

15. Harris poll conducted 26 July 2006, http://www.harrisinteractive.com/harris_poll/index.asp?PID=685. Accessed 18 November 2007.

16. Pew Research Center, "Foreign Policy Attitudes Now Driven by 9/11 and Iraq," http://people-press.org/reports/display.php3?ReportID=222. Accessed 18 November 2007.

17. Derber and Magrass, *Morality Wars*, Chapter 2.

18. Ibid. See also Jerry Lembcke, *The Spitting Image: Myth, Memory, and the Legacy of Vietnam* (New York: NYU Press, 1998).

Notes to Chapter Nine

1. Take Back America Conference, 2 June 2005, Washington, DC. Transcript of remarks available at http://www.ourfuture.org/docUploads/caf060205edwards.pdf.

2. IAFF Presidential Forum, Washington, DC, 14 March 2007, http://www.iaff.org/07News/031507ForumMedia.htm. Accessed 18 November 2007.

3. New Leadership on Healthcare Forum, Center for American Progress Action Fund, 24 March 2007, http://www.americanprogressaction.org/events/healthforum/fulltranscript.pdf. Accessed 18 November 2007.

4. Democratic Primary Debate at Saint Anselm College, 3 June 2007, http://www.boston.com/news/politics/2008/debates/060207_dem_debate_transcript. Accessed 18 November 2007.

5. Dawn Turner Trice, "Obama Unfazed by Foes' Doubts on Race Question," *Chicago Tribune*, 15 March 2004.

6. Barack Obama, *The Audacity of Hope: Thoughts on Reclaiming the American Dream* (New York: Crown, 2006), 7–9.

7. Obama, *The Audacity of Hope*, 214–216.

8. Barack Obama, "The Audacity of Hope," speech given at the 2004 Democratic National Convention. Transcript available at http://www.washingtonpost.com/wp-dyn/articles/A19751-2004Jul27.html.

9. Obama, *The Audacity of Hope*, 39–40.

10. Barack Obama, *Dreams from My Father: A Story of Race and Inheritance* (New York: Crown, 1996), 80.

11. Jeff Zeleny and Steven Greenhouse, "War on Terror Takes Focus at Democrats' Debate," *New York Times*, 8 August 2007, http://

www.nytimes.com/2007/08/08/us/politics/08dems.html. Accessed 18 November 2007.

12. Elise Labott, "Clinton, Obama in War of Words over Rogue Leaders," CNN.com/Politics, 25 July 2007, http://www.cnn.com/2007/POLITICS/07/25/clinton.obama/index.html. Accessed 18 October 2007.

13. Speech to Chicago Council on Foreign Relations, 12 July 2004.

14. Obama, *The Audacity of Hope*, 307.

15. Take Back America Conference, 20 June 2007. Transcript available at http://home.ourfuture.org/assets/tba2007-transcript-dennis_kucinich.pdf.

16. Ibid.

17. Dennis Kucinich, Response to *2008 AFL-CIO Candidate Questionnaire*, http://www.aflcio.org/issues/politics/questionnaires_denniskucinich.cfm. Accessed 18 November 2007.

18. MSNBC South Carolina 2007 Democratic Primary Debate, 26 April 2007. Transcript available at http://www.msnbc.msn.com/id/18352397/page/16.

19. Ibid.

20. Take Back America Conference, 20 June 2007. Transcript available at http://home.ourfuture.org/assets/tba2007-transcript-dennis_kucinich.pdf.

21. "Corporate Power," http://www.kucinichforcongress.com/issues/corp_power.php. Accessed 18 November 2007.

22. Take Back America Conference, 20 June 2007. Transcript available at http://home.ourfuture.org/assets/tba2007-transcript-dennis_kucinich.pdf.

23. Congressional Black Caucus Institute Debate, Baltimore, 9 September 2003. Transcript available at http://www.washingtonpost.com/wp-srv/politics/transcripts/090903debatetext.html.

24. Democratic Debate in Columbia, South Carolina, 3 May 2003. Transcript available http://www.politicallibrary.net/library/D/Debates%202004/Dems_Debate_May_3_2003.htm.

25. Ibid.

Notes to Chapter Ten

1. Ari Berman, "Edwards Money: Principle or Pragmatism?" *Nation*, 2 October 2007, http://www.thenation.com/blogs/campaignmatters?bid=45&pid=239105.

2. Hillary Clinton, *It Takes a Village* (New York: Simon and Schuster, 1996), 203.

3. Ibid., 267.

4. Ibid., 272.

5. Ibid., 279.

6. Floor Speech of First Lady Hillary Rodham Clinton at the Democratic National Convention, http://www.pbs.org/newshour/convention96/floor_speeches/hillary_clinton.html.

7. William Kristol, "How to Oppose the Health Plan—and Why," *On Principle*, January 1994, http://www.ashbrook.org/publicat/onprin/v2n1/kristol.html.

8. Campaign for America's Future, "The Progressive Majority: Why a Conservative America Is a Myth," June 2007, 23, http://mediamatters.org/progmaj/report. Accessed 15 October 2007.

9. CNN.com, "Clinton Unveils Mandatory Health Care Plan," 18 September 2007, http://www.cnn.com/2007/POLITICS/09/17/health.care/index.html.

10. Katherine Q. Seelye and Dalia Sussman, "Women Supportive but Skeptical of Clinton, Poll Says," *New York Times*, 20 July 2007, Section 1, p. 16.

11. Matthew Mosk, "Edwards Again Says He Was Wrong to Vote for War," *Washington Post*, 5 February 2007, A4.

12. Jeff Gerth and Don Van Natta Jr., "Hillary's War," *New York Times Magazine* (3 June 2007): 67.

13. Ibid., 40.

14. Patrick Healy, "Senator Clinton Speaks Up for Israel at U.N. Rally," *New York Times*, 18 July 2006, http://www.nytimes.com/2006/07/17/world/17cnd-hillary.html. Accessed 18 November 2007.

15. Robin Toner and Jeff Zeleny, "Iraq Is Flash Point as 8 Democratic Rivals Clash," *New York Times*, 4 June 2007, http://www.nytimes.com/2007/06/04/us/politics/04debate.html. Accessed 18 November 2007.

16. Jonathan Alter, "Blame America at Your Peril," *Newsweek* (15 October 2001).

17. Nina Easton, "Who Business Is Betting On," *Fortune* (9 July 2007): 45–52.

18. Ari Berman, "Hillary, Inc.," *Nation* (4 June 2007), http://www.thenation.com/doc/20070604/berman. Accessed 20 October 2007.

19. Ibid.

20. Ibid.

21. Easton, "Who Business Is Betting On," 45–52.

22. Ibid., 158–159.

23. Project Vote Smart, http://www.vote-smart.org/issue_rating_category.php?can_id=WNY99268. Accessed 20 October 2007.

24. Hillary Clinton Campaign Speech, "Economic Policy: Modern Progressive Vision, Shared Prosperity," http://www.hillaryclinton.com/news/speech/view/?id=1839. Accessed 20 October 2007.

25. Project Vote Smart, http://www.vote-smart.org/issue_rating_category.php?can_id=WNY99268. Accessed 20 October 2007.

26. Ellen Goodman, "All of a Sudden, Hillary's 'Establishment' Candidate?" *Boston Globe,* 4 October 2007.

Notes to Conclusion

1. For a discussion of the catalytic relation between the Democratic base, the Democratic Party in power, and the dynamics of regime change, see Charles Derber, *Hidden Power,* Chapter 3.

2. See Derber, *Hidden Power,* 34ff and 84–92 for a discussion of FDR's regime change and its relation to populist social movements.

3. Ibid.

4. See Charles Derber with Yale Magrass, *Morality Wars,* 145ff.

5. Ibid. See also Derber, *Hidden Power,* 38ff.

6. This is discussed extensively in Derber with Magrass, *Morality Wars,* 145ff.

7. Ibid.

8. See Derber with Magrass, *Morality Wars,* 191ff.

9. For a more extended discussion of the prospects of regime change, see Derber, *Hidden Power,* Part III.

10. See the polling data summarized in Chapter 4. See also the public opinion data discussed in Derber with Magrass, *Morality Wars,* 191ff.

11. This is discussed extensively in Matt Bai, *The Argument* (New York: Penguin, 2007).

INDEX

About the Authors

Katherine Adam is the Outreach Coordinator for the Philadelphia GROW Project, a research and advocacy organization within the Drexel University School of Public Health that serves the needs of low-income children. She has been active in Democratic Party politics at the federal, state, and local levels, including interning for Senator John Kerry. She is an honors graduate of Boston College.

Charles Derber, a noted social critic, is Professor of Sociology at Boston College. He is the author of eleven internationally acclaimed books, including *Corporation Nation, Hidden Power,* and *The Wilding of America.* He has written for the *Boston Globe, Newsday,* and other mass media, and appears frequently on television and radio talk shows. He is a longtime social activist working for democracy and social justice.